KT-573-255

A2 Business Studies

Contents

Introduction

■ ■ ■

Content Guidance

Setting corporate objectives

Tools for corporate planning

External influences

■ ■ ■

Questions and Answers

A2 Business Studies
UNIT 2880

OCR

Module 2880: Business Strategy

Roger Williams and Barry Martin

Philip Allan Updates
Market Place
Deddington
Oxfordshire
OX15 0SE

tel: 01869 338652
fax: 01869 337590
e-mail: sales@philipallan.co.uk
www.philipallan.co.uk

This Guide has been written specifically to support students preparing for the OCR Business Studies Unit 2880 examination. The content has been neither approved nor endorsed by OCR and remains the sole responsibility of the authors.

Printed by Information Press, Eynsham, Oxford

Introduction

About this guide

This book has been written with the aim of providing you with the ideal revision resource for OCR Unit 2880, A2 Business Studies. It is made up of three sections.

The first section, the **Introduction**, considers the nature and structure of the examination, the 'assessment unit'. It will help you to appreciate why the examination is structured in the way that it is, and this understanding will assist you in maximising your marks. Following a brief overview of the A2 qualification, this section focuses upon the required skills and key examination terms, concluding with revision and examination advice.

The second section, **Content Guidance**, considers the material that the examination is designed to cover. The examination can only test the content identified in the subject syllabus, the 'specification'. It is therefore important for you to know precisely what the examiners can test and what they cannot. In this way you can devote your time and energy towards the material that is relevant. There are also tips on ways to learn and understand key content. You should not view this section as an alternative textbook or a substitute for hard work in the lead-up to the examination — this guide complements consistent study.

The third section, **Questions and Answers**, provides two sample examination papers. You will receive the case studies before the examination, but only see the questions for the first time in the examination room. This section also provides sample student answers. These are analysed so that their strengths and weaknesses are clearly identified and, where appropriate, you will be shown how to improve on the answer given. Through this type of benchmarking you can improve the quality of your own answers.

Throughout this guide our focus is, unashamedly, on the objective of maximising your marks so that you can achieve the highest possible grade.

The structure of the qualification

OCR A2 Business Studies builds upon the foundation provided by OCR AS Business Studies. The A2 qualification consists of two more modules of subject content. These are assessed using three examination modules. Module 6, 2880 Business Strategy, is compulsory; its examinable content comprises the new A2 content in the module Business Strategy and all of the AS material already studied. The other two modules present you with a choice, as follows.

The first is a choice of coursework, between 2878 The Business Project and 2879 The Business Thematic Enquiry.

The second choice is one of four business behaviours to be studied in additional depth: 2874 Further Marketing, 2875 Further Accounting and Finance, 2876 Further People in Organisations and 2877 Further Operations Management.

Module 6, 2880 Business Strategy, is very important within the structure of the A2 qualification. It is the synoptic unit. This means it assesses the ability to explain, analyse and evaluate the whole subject. This requires thinking in an integrated and strategic manner, viewing problems as multi-disciplinary rather than discretely behavioural. As the specification states:

> The emphasis is on strategic understanding and on the ability to draw evidence together from any relevant area of the syllabus. Assessment focuses on the breadth, depth and quality of the candidate's analysis and evaluation.

Assessment

The A2 qualification is designed to test certain skills. Consequently, in order to gain marks, candidates have to demonstrate these skills. The skills form a hierarchy, from 'knowledge' at the lowest level to 'evaluation' at the highest.

- **Knowledge** — the ability to recall accurately subject ideas and concepts.
- **Application** — bringing subject knowledge to bear on a situation.
- **Analysis** — the development of an argument that shows reasoning and a chain of logic using appropriate concepts and techniques of business studies.
- **Evaluation** — making a reasoned judgement having considered the available evidence critically.

These are the same skills that were developed in the AS qualification. However, their relative weighting changes. At A2 greater emphasis is placed upon being able to evaluate rather than merely recall knowledge. For this module, 2880 Business Strategy, the weighting is:

- **Knowledge** 20%
- **Application** 23¾%
- **Analysis** 26¼%
- **Evaluation** 30%

To gain 70% or more of the marks for a question you must be able to demonstrate the skill of evaluation in your answer. If you can do this, the examiner will assume that you have acquired all of the three preceding skills regardless of whether you display them or not.

This module, Business Strategy, will have four questions. There will be 76 marks for business studies (with a further 4 marks for the quality of written communication). For example, if a question is worth 20 marks then the mark allocation will be:

- Level 4   Evaluation   (15–20)
- Level 3   Analysis   (9–14)
- Level 2   Application   (4–8)
- Level 1   Knowledge   (1–3)

Hence, demonstration of knowledge alone would gain a maximum of 3 marks. In contrast, because the skills are hierarchical, the demonstration of evaluation would gain at least 15 marks. The awarding of the precise number of marks within a mark range is a matter for the examiner's professional judgement about the quality of the skill being demonstrated.

At AS the way to see the highest skill that the question required was to look at both the key verb and mark allocation. This synoptic unit is different: every question will have marks allocated for evaluation. This makes what you have to do in the examination room less complicated: you must demonstrate the highest possible level of skill required by all the questions, i.e. evaluation.

Pre-issued case study

The case study for 2880 Business Strategy is pre-issued. The questions are seen for the first time in the examination room. This approach will be familiar to you as it was used at AS for 2873 Business Behaviour.

The case material will cover all aspects of the course: the internal workings of organisations (marketing, accounting and finance, people in organisations, operations management) and the external dynamic environment they operate in. Consequently, it is not possible to revise selectively. Further, your revision should also cover all the AS material.

When the case material arrives, tackle it systematically. First, photocopy it. Treat one copy as your working copy. The second, clean, copy is security in case you lose the first. Further, having a clean copy means you can assess your understanding of the case without the aid of the notes you will have made on your working copy. Remember, you cannot take your own copy into the examination room.

Next, read the case. The aim of this first read-through is to gain a broad overview of the context of the organisation. Having read the case, you should now aim to read it again, but this time with the specific intention of gaining a greater understanding. The case is written to provide a context on which questions can be set to assess the specification. So, as you read through the case for the second, and each subsequent time, try to identify the main specification areas that are suggested. The emphasis should be on identifying the broad issues, not specific questions.

Being both synoptic and strategic, the case material will visit each of the four internal behaviours. For example, there might be reference to aggressive competition from imports. This might suggest the firm needs to review its strategic approach to marketing, looking at its product portfolio, customers' views of the product and the possible need for additional product attributes, the price sensitivity of customers in case the competitor lowers prices, the effect of a strengthening of sterling, and so on. The case study provides the context and evidence on which you can and should draw to support your answers in the examination.

Case studies are set some time in advance of the examination date. This means the appropriateness of any historic data can be improved by research into how the data may have changed since the case was written. In your answers, try to incorporate evidence of an appreciation of the current environment and issues likely to face the type of business that forms the context of the case. For example, how might the current macroeconomic climate affect the type of organisation in the case? Use the pre-issue time to research the context.

Revision planning

The way you plan your revision is essentially down to personal preference, as what may work for one individual may not work for another. However, there are common principles of revision that lead to examination success.

- Start your revision in plenty of time. This means you need to know the date of the examination well in advance.
- Ensure that your notes and files are complete.
- Ensure you have an appropriate textbook and identify which sections are relevant by checking against your scheme of work.
- Arrange to have somewhere quiet and comfortable to work. Try to avoid being disturbed while you are studying.
- Set yourself a series of short-term goals within an overall revision schedule.
- Reward yourself as you reach short-term goals by taking a few minutes away from revision.
- Work in short, intense, bursts. Quality of revision is as important as quantity.
- Reread your notes. Jotting down the key points as you read will help maintain concentration. Try using mind maps/diagrams rather than continuous prose.
- Make a note of any areas of uncertainty so you can ask for clarification later.
- Practise writing answers to examination questions without your notes and within the time limit of the examination.
- Check your answers to ensure that they contain the higher-order skills.
- The night before the examination, read through the case once more, using your clean, unannotated copy, to ensure you are not overly dependent on your notes.

Examination success

Sitting examinations can be a stressful experience. However, stress can be alleviated by appropriate preparation. As a minimum you will need to:

- know the date, time and location of the examination
- arrive at least 10 minutes before the scheduled start time
- ensure that you have all of your examination equipment, i.e. black pens, pencils and a ruler and calculator
- know what demands the examiner will make of you
- become familiar with the examination format, i.e. number and style of questions
- know what you can achieve in the time permitted
- make sure you write clearly, using sentences that are not too long and clumsy

Because the case study is pre-issued, you should have a robust understanding of all of the case material whether it be verbal, numerate or graphical. Further, you should have already assimilated the key issues facing the organisation, the chronology, personalities and any specialist vocabulary. So, begin by reading the questions. Read each carefully. Pay particular attention to new information, names, events or key phrases. Now read through the case study again. This time, the aim is to identify how the new information, names, events or key phrases link to the case material.

During the second read-through, identify which aspects of the case are fact and which are opinion, which events have already taken place and which are anticipated. Opinions and anticipation are important, but they need to be regarded with greater caution than facts and history when they are used to support an answer.

All four questions are compulsory. There is no requirement to answer them in any particular order. Whatever order you choose to answer them, it is vital that you answer all four completely, giving each an appropriate amount of time, effort and attention. Unless there are good reasons to do otherwise, it would seem sensible to answer them in number sequence. This is simply because this approach minimises the risk of missing out a question.

The A2 specification, like the AS, contains quantitative techniques and tools for decision-making, for example break-even analysis. The A2 specification also introduces new quantitative techniques, e.g. decision trees. Although there will not be a question explicitly requiring the quantitative analysis of a situation, or the use of a particular quantitative technique, this does not mean these are unimportant. Rather, the tools and techniques should be used as often as is appropriate. The outcome of a calculation will provide further evidence to use in an answer. The examiner will be seeking to reward the use of the technique. But the examiner will be interested in how it has been used rather than slavishly adhering to a single possible answer. By definition, quantitative tools are analytical and so their use will attract a high proportion of the marks. Good qualitative discussion, which evaluates the usefulness of the tool or its outcome, would result in a top grade. In essence, rather than be worried about quantitative analysis, embrace it as a route to high marks.

The examination for Business Strategy lasts 120 minutes. Allow about 10 minutes to read the questions and to make a rough answer plan for each. With 80 marks available you should aim to be working at a pace of just under $1\frac{1}{2}$ minutes per mark — hence a 20-mark question should take less than 30 minutes. Remember, the quality of your written communication will be assessed, so it is important to pay attention to sentence and paragraph construction as well as basic spelling, punctuation and grammar.

Finally, gaining the top grade requires three things, all equally important:
(1) Being utterly rigorous in answering the question set by the examiner. During the pre-issue time, you will have identified a broad range of issues facing the organisation. But in the examination your focus must be solely on the ones selected by

the examiner. No matter how good your answer is, it can only be rewarded if it answers the question set. So, read the questions with extreme care. Identify the key aspect of the specification being assessed. Start your answer by giving a brief definition of it. Be ruthless in ensuring that the rest of your answer is relevant.

(2) Demonstrating a high level of skill in the examination. As already explained, your answer must be evaluative if you are to secure a top grade.

(3) Subject understanding. This is something you will have been building since the start of the AS course. You must enter the examination room with a secure and robust understanding of the entire course, knowing, for example, how the organisation would be affected by a given change in its macroeconomic environment.

Content
Guidance

The content of the unit divides into six major areas:

- Setting corporate objectives (pages 13–16)
- Tools for corporate planning (pages 16–24)
- External influences (pages 24–35)
- Devising and implementing strategy (pages 35–42)
- Reviewing strategy (pages 42–46)
- Managing strategic change (pages 46–52)

Although you may well have studied each area separately, the emphasis in this module is on integration and strategic thinking. The specification states:

> The unifying theme is choosing and justifying strategy and as such candidates are expected to demonstrate an analytical and evaluative approach to the content introduced in this module *and to that from the AS modules*. (authors' emphasis)

This means you should revisit the work you covered for AS as part of your revision for this unit. In doing this, your aim should be to gain an evaluative appreciation of the material, rather than merely factual recall.

The specification guidance continues:

> The emphasis should be on strategy, its nature, development, implementation and critical evaluation in the context of specific organisational and business situations. Hence candidates are required to recognise potential conflict between the objectives of different stakeholder interests and suggest and evaluate resolutions to such conflicts. They should be able to recognise the inter-relationships between objectives and an uncertain business environment and to devise and evaluate strategies, which aim to anticipate, respond to and manage change. Candidates are required to demonstrate their integrative understanding of the subject and to be able to approach situations from the perspective of different stakeholders.

This means you should be able to discuss business problems from more than one viewpoint. For example, if the issue is location, then you should be able to discuss not only the operations management issues but also others. These might include sources of finance, severance, recruitment, selection and training of employees, to identify a few. In addition the impact of a change of location upon the interested stakeholder groups, such as the community, suppliers and owners, should be considered.

Setting corporate objectives

Strategy

What is strategy?

So what is strategy? It would seem sensible to have a robust understanding of the term before proceeding. Although there are several definitions, they each have common themes. In essence we can define strategy as:

- the direction of the organisation
- towards common objectives
- which results in long-term advantage
- by blending the integration of internal resources
- within the pressures and constraints afforded by a dynamic external environment
- to meet the needs of stakeholders, e.g. customers, employees and owners

Key features of strategy

This gives rise to three features of strategy:

- using resources to achieve a sustainable competitive advantage
- a critical understanding of the external environment, i.e. whether it is stable or turbulent
- the transformational process, i.e. strategy adds value for the benefit of stakeholders

Formulating strategy

Formulating strategy has three parts:

- **analysis** — identification of what needs to be done within the given situation
- **development** — deciding how it is to be done
- **implementation** — turning the plan into action, i.e. doing it

These stages can either be carried out **sequentially**:

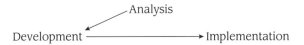

or, **concurrently**:

Setting strategy sequentially is most suited to situations with little, or gradual, environmental change because it does not allow for easy adaptation once begun. In contrast, although more challenging, concurrent strategy formulation allows for situations of greater uncertainty, either environmental or objective.

Good strategy

A good strategy is one that:

- delivers increased value to stakeholders
- is consistent with the resources and environment
- gives the organisation some sustainable distinctive ability or competitive advantage

Evaluation A strategy will only be appropriate in a particular set of circumstances. Whether the strategy adopted is the right one is therefore highly situational. So, a change in the external environment may render a chosen strategy ineffective. Similarly, a reassessment of stakeholder objectives would lead to a re-evaluation of the chosen strategy.

Whether strategy should be formulated sequentially or concurrently depends upon the degree of turbulence and the abilities of those involved in the process. Always remember that decision-makers formulate strategy. Being concerned with the future, which is itself uncertain, decision-makers have to employ judgements. Such judgements will reflect their own values and beliefs. Further, the identified strategy is implemented through people. Thus to be effective the strategy has to be communicated and understood by all those involved in its delivery.

Corporate objectives

The objectives of an organisation reflect its goal. The goal is the general statement of the organisation's intent. So, objectives are more precise statements of where the organisation wants to be. They are often quantified. Objectives are, in turn, the basis for the setting of more detailed targets.

Objectives serve to:

- provide a means of assessing progress
- communicate a sense of purpose within the organisation
- facilitate coordination

To have a motivational impact, the objectives need to be:

- clearly understood
- congruent with the culture of the organisation
- challenging yet achievable

Evaluation The validity of objectives will depend upon the resources available within the organisation, the nature of the environment and the values and beliefs of the key stakeholders. Without clear objectives it is impossible to have a meaningful strategy.

Formation of objectives

Individuals set objectives. Different individuals will have different agendas and interests for the organisation. Consequently the emerging objectives for the organisation will depend upon stakeholder analysis and organisational culture and mission.

Stakeholder analysis

What is it that each stakeholder group wants, and how influential are they in a given set of circumstances? This can be shown diagrammatically:

		Level of interest	
		Low	**High**
Power	**Low**	Little influence	Emphasis is on communication, telling them what is happening and why
	High	Emphasis is on maintaining satisfaction	Key players

Organisational culture and mission

Culture reflects the organisation's ability to be innovative and to accept risk. These two factors will in turn influence the organisation's ability to embark upon change.

Evaluation The power of stakeholders will influence objectives. For example, the power of shareholders will be dependent upon the degree of fragmentation of ownership. Shareholders might be influential in a private limited company with a few major shareholders but less so for a public limited company (plc) with, potentially, millions of shareholders each holding a very few shares.

The important stakeholders are those who express and show a high degree of interest in the progress of the organisation and have the ability to exert influence by virtue of their power. This combination of interest and power has the potential to make the media a key stakeholder group, for example. Similarly, a trade union with a high degree of membership density becomes a key player if its actions could cause severe disruption, for example when there is high demand but low stocks of finished goods.

Communication of objectives

Corporate plans and mission statements

A mission statement sets out the overriding purpose of an organisation. It is a broadly worded expression of where the organisation intends to go and the reasoning that underpins it. The statement communicates purpose to stakeholders.

To be effective the mission statement should:
- give the nature of the organisation, e.g. what market it serves
- set out its basic values and beliefs
- suggest how a sustainable competitive advantage will emerge
- be drafted so that stakeholders understand it
- indicate why the mission matters

Evaluation The relevance of a mission statement depends upon the degree to which it reflects the values and expectations of the stakeholders. Because strategy is implemented through people, the mission will be achieved only if those affected by it are in agreement with what it sets out to do.

Stakeholder objectives

Stakeholder objectives and the firm's decisions

Differing stakeholders will have differing interests in the organisation and these interests will change through time. What the organisation does, and how it does it, will be influenced by its stakeholders and their ability to exert influence. To be successful in the long term, the organisation has to achieve a balance between these often conflicting stakeholder objectives. Therefore stakeholder power and influence have to be analysed and understood by those responsible for strategy formulation.

Evaluation No one single stakeholder group is the most influential; their influence is situational.

Tools for corporate planning

Managers take decisions that relate to some future period of time. Since there will be a time interval between taking the decision and its implementation, managers need to understand and anticipate how the organisation's environment will change. Consequently, decisions contain risk.

Managers use a variety of tools and techniques to help them to minimise the negative impact of uncertainty. Some of these tools are studied for AS, e.g. investment appraisal and break even as a decision-making tool. Similarly, the concepts of product life cycle and portfolio analysis are aids to decision-making that could legitimately be used in answers at A2.

The A2 specification introduces five new tools to aid decision-making. Because of the nature of the unit examination (its synoptic requirement), a question cannot demand the explicit use of any individual decision tool. However, the context and the data might suggest that using a particular tool would be appropriate. By their very nature, these tools are analytical so their use will attract a high percentage of the available marks. You should be confident in their use, suitability and limitations.

Ansoff's matrix

This is essentially a marketing based tool. However, it can be applied at a whole organisation level, particularly in the context of conglomerate businesses. The matrix relates the organisation to the markets in which it operates. It considers two dimensions: products and markets. For Ansoff's matrix to be useful to decision-makers, they have to understand these two dimensions:

- 'Market' describes a customer.
- 'Product' describes what the organisation sells to a customer. So, a single customer might buy several different products.

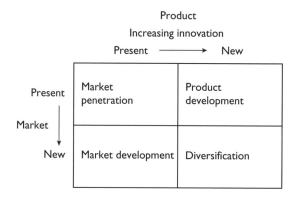

Some strategic actions carry greater risk than others. For example, continuing to sell the same product to the same customers, market penetration, is intrinsically less risky than developing a new product for a new customer base, diversification. Essentially risk increases with movement away from the familiar, whether product or market.

> **Evaluation** Ansoff's matrix offers a way of generating options, but it does not provide the decision-maker with guidance as to which option may be the best. Assessing the suitability of an option requires other strategic and analytical techniques. Hence, the matrix provides a structure for strategic decision-making rather than a solution.

Decision trees

A decision tree is a diagram that sets out the various possible outcomes to a series of sequential decisions where there is an element of chance. The specification states that you need to be able both to draw and to evaluate a decision tree.

Constructing a decision tree

The tree has three components:

- ——— **a branch** — these are drawn as lines

- ○ **an event node** (something the decision-maker has no control over, i.e. a chance event) — these are drawn as circles

- ▢ **a decision node** (the decision-maker is able to select which branch of the tree to follow) — these are drawn as squares

A financial value is attached to each individual branch. This value is then multiplied by the estimated probability of the outcome occurring. The result is known as the Expected Monetary Value (EMV). The EMV of all the branches leading into an event node is summed. When drawing a tree, check that all the probabilities of the branches leading into an event node total 100%.

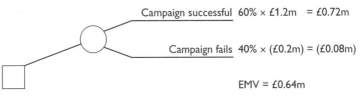

Campaign successful 60% × £1.2m = £0.72m

Campaign fails 40% × (£0.2m) = (£0.08m)

EMV = £0.64m

Using a decision tree

At a decision node the EMVs of the branches leading into it are compared. The branches leading into a decision node do not have probabilities because they represent alternative courses of actions and not chance events. The decision tree guides the decision-maker towards what is the most favourable outcome by selecting the branch with the highest EMV.

Launch campaign £0.64m

Update product £0.60m

Here, the EMV of the campaign exceeds the EMV of updating the product, so the tree guides the decision-maker to the advertising campaign (the branch not selected is crossed through).

Evaluation The outcome of the tree will depend on the data used. The reliability of the data is, therefore, a key issue. Changing the probability or financial value of a branch will change its EMV. Hence, a major strategic decision would be subject to different assumptions if changes were made to the data. By making such changes the decision-maker can assess how sensitive the decision is to changed conditions and assumptions.

When using a decision tree always consider the accuracy of the data and, in the context of the case study, where the data came from. It might be that the person providing the data wants a particular decision to be made — how objective are the data? Second, look at the difference between the EMVs of the branches leading into a decision node. The closer they are, the less clear cut is the decision. Close EMVs should be commented upon in an evaluative manner.

Time series analysis (TSA)

Time series analysis is a technique that uses historic data to forecast possible future events. It is typically used in forecasting sales levels from data about previous sales (but it need not be confined to this context). The underlying assumption for TSA is that past behaviour will continue into the future. Hence, it is most appropriate when:

- there are few environmental changes, i.e. steady conditions
- trying to forecast in the short term

Moving averages

By using moving averages, historic data are broken down into three components:

- trend
- cyclical variation
- random component

When faced with a set of data, the first decision you will need to make is the number of data points to include in the moving average. (Remember, the examiner cannot demand that you use TSA. Therefore, the examiner cannot tell you to use, for example, a three-point moving average.) The aim is to use a moving average that corresponds to the pattern in the data. The pattern in the data will suggest which moving average will produce the smoothest trend line. A pattern that repeats itself every three data points is best smoothed using a three-point moving average. Similarly, a pattern that repeats itself every four data points is best smoothed using a four-point moving average.

The more data points in the moving average:

- the smoother the trend line
- the shorter the trend line

Trend

By calculating a moving average, the trend is produced. The trend is plotted on graph paper. The appropriate moving average will produce a trend line that is both smooth and sufficiently long to allow it to be extended with confidence. The extended trend yields the forecast trend. But, because the decision-maker will want to know sales, the trend has to be adjusted by allowing for the cyclical variation.

Cyclical variation

The cyclical variation (CV) is the regular movements of the data from the trend. It is calculated as:

CV = data – trend

Because the data may not follow a precisely repeated pattern, it is necessary to determine the average CV for each stage in the cycle. The average CV is then added to the forecast trend to yield the forecast sales.

The following example illustrates the use of TSA. By examining the data, it can be seen that they follow a clear pattern across three data points, so a three-point moving average is used to produce a smooth trend line.

Data	Stage in cycle	Moving average trend	CV (data – trend)
112	1		
109	2	113.00	–4.00
118	3	116.00	2.00
121	1	119.00	2.00
118	2	122.00	–4.00
127	3	124.67	2.33
129	1	127.33	1.67
126	2		

The average CV can now be found for each stage. (*Note:* there are two CVs for each stage in the cycle.)

(1) $(2.00 + 1.67)/2 = 3.67/2 = 1.84$

(2) $(-4.00 + -4.00)/2 = -8.00/2 = -4.00$

(3) $(2.00 + 2.33)/2 = 4.33/2 = 2.17$

By plotting and extending the trend, you get a forecast trend for the next three data points. The forecast trend is then adjusted by the average CV for that stage in the cycle to give the forecast sales.

Forecast trend (A)	Average CV (B)	Stage in cycle	Forecast sales (C)	Forecast A + B = C (to nearest whole number)
132.7	2.17	3	134.87	135
135.0	1.84	1	136.84	137
137.3	–4.00	2	133.30	133

Random component

By definition, the third element of TSA, the random component, cannot be predicted. Hence, no allowance is made for it other than the recognition that any forecast is subject to a degree of error.

Evaluation As with any technique, the appropriateness of TSA depends on the reliability of the data. Similarly, the reliability and robustness of the forecast depends upon:

- the amount of variation in the original data
- how far into the future one tries to forecast (TSA is best used as a short-term method)
- the amount of data available

Because TSA uses a judgemental extension of a plotted line, the forecast trend is prone to error. Offering three versions for each future data point — pessimistic, neutral and optimistic — can offset this weakness. So rather than offer a single forecast, the decision-maker should work within a range of possibilities. Also, because TSA provides the decision-maker with a number, and one that may be quoted to a number of decimal places, there is a danger that the number will be treated as fact. TSA doesn't forecast what will happen. Rather it forecasts what might happen given no external change (e.g. a change in a competitor's price) or internal change (e.g. a change in product quality). This technique is therefore best employed in situations of little environmental change.

Gathering information and summarising data

Data are a vital requirement for informed decision-making. Without data the manager is reduced to making guesses and the success of the organisation is reduced to chance.

There is a subtle difference between information and data. Information is measurement, e.g. the number of sales made last month. The processing of information turns it into data useful for decision-making, e.g. the percentage change in sales last month. The task for the decision-maker is to analyse the data.

Collecting information

This section clearly builds upon the foundations laid at AS, particularly regarding market research. However, marketing is not the only context in which data might be required. Others include labour turnover, scrap rates and trends in debtor collection period. To be appropriate, the method of information-collection has to reflect:

- why the data are required
- when they are needed by
- what form they are required in
- who wants them

Methods of collecting information range from casual conversation with other managers, observation, surveys, consumer panels and so on, through to detailed market analysis combining several methods. The more important the nature of the decision, and the greater the consequences of taking the wrong decision, the more formalised and structured the information-gathering process should be.

Summarising data

The skills of summarising data are useful and appropriate in many different contexts. To be useful for decision-making the information gathered has to be translated into data. So, summarising information about an ice-cream manufacturer selling to both supermarkets and wholesalers might yield the following data:

- **averages**, i.e. mean, median, mode (e.g. mean monthly sales)
- **spread**, i.e. width or range (e.g. summer vs winter sales levels)
- **percentage**, i.e. change and proportion (e.g. 75% of sales are made to 5% of customers)
- **trends**, i.e. movement within information (e.g. sales rise faster in summer than winter)
- **correlation**, i.e. a causal linkage between two variables (e.g. sales rise with temperature)

Critical path analysis (CPA)

CPA is essentially a resource allocation model. It can be used in situations when the manager is faced with a complex task, a project, which can be broken down into a number of interrelated subtasks or activities.

Benefits of CPA

Determination of the critical path enables the manager to find the shortest time in which the project can be completed. Further, the manager can identify the earliest time each activity in the project can start. The manager thus knows when the necessary resources have to be available so that the project can continue on schedule. This avoids acquiring resources too soon only to have them sitting idle, absorbing capital. Also, identifying when resources will be needed means they can be ordered to arrive just-in-time (JIT). Hence, CPA links to JIT.

Another benefit of CPA is that it identifies which activities in a project are time sensitive. These activities have to start and finish on time if the project is to be completed to schedule. This enables the manager to prioritise activities. In turn, management attention, another resource, can be focused on those activities with high priority. Activities that are time sensitive are called 'critical activities'. Any delay in a critical activity will delay the entire project.

Constructing a network

CPA divides a project into two components: nodes and activities.
- **Nodes** show the start and finish of activities.
- **Activities** are things that require time and resources. They are shown as arrows, and the arrowheads join to the nodes.

The use of nodes and activities shows the logical relationships within a project. These are the building blocks of a network.

When drawing a network remember:
- All networks start with a single node.
- All networks end with a single node.
- Arrowheads show the sequence of activities; it is impossible to evaluate a network if the arrowheads are not drawn.
- Activities should not cross.

Analysing a network

- First, work from left to right to calculate the Earliest Start Time (EST) and Earliest Finish Time (EFT).
- The EST of activities from the start node is zero. If two or more activities emerge from the start node, they all have the same EST, zero.
- The EFT of an activity is its own EST plus its own duration:

    EFT = EST + duration

- The EST of the next activity is the EFT of the preceding activity.
- When an activity is dependent on more than one preceding activity, its EST is the largest EFT.
- The EFT of a network is the largest EFT of the activities leading into the end node.
- Now work from right to left to calculate the Latest Finish Time (LFT) and the Latest Start Time (LST).
- The LFT of activities leading into the end nodes is the project's duration. All activities leading into the end node have the same LFT.
- The LST of an activity is its own LFT minus its own duration:

    LST = LFT – duration

- The LFT of the preceding activity is the LST of the next activity.
- When an activity precedes more than one following activity, its LFT is the smallest EST of the following activities.
- For each activity, calculate Total Float (TF) and Free Float (FF) to identify the critical activities:

    TF = LST – EST = LTF – EFT
    FF = EST of the next activity – activity duration – its own EST

Interpreting float

- Any activity can be delayed up to its Total Float without delaying the whole project.
- Any overrun on the Total Float on any activity will cause the project to overrun.
- Any activity can be delayed up to its Free Float without delaying the start of the next activity.
- If Total Float is zero, Free Float must be zero.

    Evaluation Although CPA highlights the more important activities in a project, all activities still have to be completed. CPA alerts the manager to the time schedule both of the activities and of the project as a whole. The completion of the activities requires the allocation of resources by the manager to optimise the project's completion. Typically the resources under the manager's control will be financial and people. Moving people from one activity to another involves consideration of their different skills and the impact on the motivation of the employees concerned. Any change may impact negatively on the duration of an activity. The role of the manager in instigating this change within the schedule is crucial if the paper-based evaluation of the network is to materialise as a completed project.

External influences

This section of the specification revisits many of the influences first encountered in Module 2871: Businesses, Their Objectives and Environment. The major difference is that at A2 the emphasis is on being able to evaluate how a particular external influence affects the behaviour of a particular firm. It is not enough to be able to identify the general impact. It is also necessary to show how the firm being studied might be affected and how it might change its behaviour as a result. Consequently, reference must always be made to the business in the case study.

The market

Market failure

A market is said to 'fail' when it is unable to allocate the resources within it effectively because of some imperfections. Examples of imperfections include the presence of large employers, such as the government, e.g. in teaching and medical care, and large employee groupings, such as trade unions. Similarly, the presence within a market of a dominant customer or dominant supplier will cause market imperfections.

Other examples of market failure include the existence of negative externalities, e.g. the social costs, such as pollution, associated with a business activity.

Government intervention

Government intervenes in markets in an attempt to compensate for or correct market failure. For example, government intervenes, through competition legislation, to prevent firms becoming monopoly providers within their market. Monopolies impact upon various stakeholder groups. For example, a monopoly provider might reduce consumer sovereignty by being able to raise price or restrict choice, and by failing to innovate. Consequently, the government legislates to prevent the formation of monopolies and the creation of anti-competitive practices so as to promote competition within product markets.

Similarly, government intervenes in the labour market to reduce exploitation of employees: measures include the National Minimum Wage, various acts concerned with employment protection as well as the Working Time Directive.

Stakeholder responses

Any business transaction will create an externality. Most measures to reduce externalities use the law, e.g. planning permission for new building, or fines for polluting. However, the increasing ability of media pressure and the threat of adverse publicity are now making businesses more responsive to their communities. Similarly, employees, with the support of trade union expertise and legislation, are less tolerant of inadequate health and safety provision in the workplace.

Evaluation The extent to which a business is responsive to stakeholder pressure to correct market failure is dependent upon the relative powers of the business and of the stakeholder group concerned. Large businesses are able to lobby the government in an attempt to create a legislative framework that is more favourable to them. This may be at the expense of the interests of other stakeholders. However, this advantage may be short-lived as customers, employees and others seek to counteract business influence.

Labour markets

Businesses hire labour because they need skills to produce an output. Therefore, the quantity of skill required is closely linked to the demand for the business's products. As demand rises, so will the need for labour unless the existing labour can become more productive. But, because of the considerable financial costs and the legislative framework associated with changing the size of a labour force, firms will only embark on such change if the need is thought to be long term. An alternative approach is to have a flexible labour force that can supply varying amounts of labour as demand for the product fluctuates. The firm's ability to secure such flexibility will reflect the characteristics of the local labour market.

Impact of skills shortages and surpluses

The less durable and storable the product, the more closely the demand for the product is linked to the demand for labour. Hence, in the service sector (e.g. hairdressing) an increase in demand for haircuts will lead to a rapid increase in the demand for labour. This can be achieved in the following ways:
(1) By hiring extra stylists if the upturn in demand is judged to be long term.
(2) If the increase is viewed as being temporary, or of a short-term cyclical nature, then the amount of output produced by existing stylists needs to be raised. This can be achieved by each stylist either working more hours or working more efficiently, both of which carry a potential risk to quality.

The more skill required in an occupation, the lower will be the degree of fluctuation in supply. Three factors explain this.

(1) Skills arise in part because firms have invested in the education and training of staff. Because of this investment, firms will be reluctant to lose trained staff.

(2) The greater the skill, the smaller is its supply in the labour market. Firms will experience difficulty in recruitment of these scarce skills.

(3) A skilled worker can always undertake a role that does not demand the particular specialist skill. However, the reverse is not true of an unskilled worker. Hence, if head count is to be reduced, unskilled staff are both easier and cheaper to replace.

> **Evaluation** How a business responds to changes in the labour market will depend upon the ability of the firm to change the composition of its labour force. This ability to respond will reflect the skill of the staff required. The greater the degree of skill required within an occupation, the lower is the willingness of the business to hire and fire. Further, the more important the continuity of personal service with customers, the less replaceable these staff become.

Unemployment

Unemployment exists when there are more people of working age in the labour market than there are job opportunities.

Types of unemployment

Types, and causes, of unemployment include:
- structural — changes in the role of primary and secondary industries
- cyclical — movements within the business cycle, e.g. recession
- regional — geographical immobility of labour
- seasonal — demand is linked to the time of year, e.g. agricultural work
- frictional — short time periods between leaving one job and finding another

Impact of unemployment on firms

Unemployment impacts upon firms in two principal ways.

Demand for the firm's output

As unemployment rises, average incomes fall. This will mean a reduction in demand for goods and services. Similarly, the threat of unemployment may cause a reduction in consumer confidence that in turn will reduce overall demand. Firms producing goods for which the demand is income-sensitive, or the suppliers to such firms, will be most affected. However, businesses that sell locally, e.g. hairdressers, may not experience much change in demand if regional unemployment does not rise.

Supply and cost of labour

Rising unemployment will reduce upward pressure on wages. This will be especially so if there is regional unemployment and the workforce does not have a unique skill.

> **Evaluation** The extent of the impact of unemployment on a firm will reflect the degree to which those unemployed can replace those in work. This, in turn, will depend upon skill levels of both the employed and the unemployed, as well as the level of regional unemployment. In addition, depending upon the nature of the firm's output, demand may fall due to a reduction in disposable incomes.

Interest, exchange and taxation rates

The impact of these economic factors on a firm's competitiveness is both internal and external.

Internal impact

Internally, a change in an economic factor will impact upon the firm's cost structure.

Changes in the exchange rate

An increase in the value of sterling against other currencies will mean that imported raw materials become cheaper in sterling, thus reducing unit cost. The extent to which the exchange rate impacts upon a firm's costs will reflect the portion of unit costs accounted for by raw materials and the size of the exchange rate movement.

Changes in interest rates

In contrast, a rise in interest rates will increase the interest charge in the profit and loss account on any variable rate borrowing. Hence, a rise in interest rates will serve to increase the costs of firms in debt, whether a short-term overdraft or longer-term loan. For firms with no debt, or those with large cash deposits, a rise in interest rates would be beneficial in terms of the additional interest accruing. Thus, the same external change can impact on firms in differing ways.

Changes in taxation

Similarly, the analysis for a change in taxation would need to consider the nature of the tax and the extent of the change. An increase in corporation tax would reduce profits to shareholders and so reduce the attractiveness of investments. However, the impact of a rise in indirect tax, e.g. VAT, would depend upon the extent to which the business could pass on this extra cost to its customers. This ability will depend upon the price sensitivity (price elasticity of demand) of the firm's market.

External impact

Externally all of the above changes in the economic environment will impact upon customers and competitors.

Changes in the exchange rate

The change in exchange rates might make an imported product more price-competitive if the advantage of the currency appreciation is passed on to the customer. Exchange rate movements will not automatically lead to price changes, particularly in markets where loyalty is a major issue. In some markets the importer might use the currency appreciation as a means of securing higher profit margins or as an opportunity to increase other product attributes, e.g. additional features at no additional uplift in price.

Changes in interest rates and taxation

Similarly, changes in interest rates and taxation will affect the disposable income of customers. Because of the high incidence of owner occupation in the UK, changes in interest rates have a significant impact on disposable incomes through mortgage payments. This may then affect demand for goods which are particularly income sensitive. However, if the firm's market comprises people who are mainly net savers, e.g. the retired, then an increase in interest rates might lead to an increase in demand, e.g. for Saga holidays.

In the same way, changes in taxation will only affect those who pay tax. It is necessary to consider the nature of the tax and the nature of the market. Increases in VAT will affect everyone purchasing the product. However, increases in PAYE will not affect those below the minimum tax threshold, e.g. those on low incomes or indeed those working in the hidden economy.

Evaluation In evaluating the impact of an economic change it is necessary to analyse the firm's situation. The major issues to consider are the competitive characteristics of the market, whether there is existing or potential competition, and the nature of the customer base. A further issue is whether the changed economic circumstance is temporary or permanent. Strategic decisions are concerned with the long run and so a strategic reaction will require the expectation that the observed change is going to be sustained. For example, before deciding to abandon an export market because of exchange rate movements, the firm would need to form the view that the long-term prognosis of operating in that market is poor.

Inflation and deflation

Inflation: causes and cures; impact upon the firm

Inflation is the tendency for the general price level to rise so that there is a reduction in the purchasing power of money.

The two types of inflation are:
- cost-push — businesses seek to pass on rising costs to the customer through higher prices
- demand-pull — customer demand outstrips supply, so enabling producers to increase price without reducing sales

Inflation can be beneficial to a business because it allows the business to raise prices, thus reducing the need to focus upon efficiency. Similarly, through price rises the profit margins on raw material will increase. Further, the real cost of loan repayments will be eroded.

However, inflation creates uncertainty, both for the business and for its customers. In a climate of rising prices, accurate business forecasting becomes much more problematic. Consequently, investment spending is less likely and firms will be less willing to advance credit to customers. Similarly, customers will lose confidence and as such may become more aware of price.

Deflation

Deflation is the persistent tendency for prices generally to fall. It is much rarer than inflation. Some economists consider that Japan is currently undergoing deflation and fear this may happen in the West. With prices falling, the prospects for profitability appear to diminish as costs may not fall so fast. Businesses are unwilling to invest or expand. Despite the fact that central banks may cut interest rates almost to zero, businesses and consumers will not borrow because confidence is low.

> **Evaluation** In a period of almost stable prices, businesses can plan ahead with greater transparency because price or cost changes are 'real' and are not due purely to inflation.

Economic growth

The five major macroeconomic objectives of government are:
- stable exchange rates
- a high level of employment
- reduced inequality of income
- price stability, defined as annual inflation of 2.5%
- economic growth

Economic growth is measured by changes in real gross domestic product (GDP). The government aims for growth at 2.5% p.a. This level of growth is regarded as sustainable in the long run without causing inflationary pressures, i.e. it produces a steady upward trend, rather than the severe fluctuation of boom, recession and slump in the business cycle. To achieve this aim, various policy instruments will be used, e.g. monetary policy.

Effects on business activity and strategic decision-making

Growth affects businesses in a variety of ways. Generally, growth is accompanied by consumer confidence and hence rising demand. How growth affects a firm will reflect the nature of its output and in particular whether it is income sensitive. Thus, producers of luxury goods will experience a greater change in demand than those providing a necessity. Luxury goods providers may therefore decide to increase output and so in turn recruit and select more labour. However, this may be difficult if growth is accompanied by lower unemployment, caused by other firms similarly hiring labour so as to increase output.

Growth may also lead to an increase in import substitution, particularly if domestic producers are unwilling or unable to satisfy rising demand. Rising imports could lead to a current account deficit and so prompt government intervention.

Evaluation Growth provides many opportunities for businesses to achieve their objective of profit. However, the ability to make profits will encourage additional firms into markets and so lead to increased competition. The extent to which competition increases will reflect the ease with which firms can enter new markets, i.e. the level of barriers to entry. Increased activity will also mean that securing resources will become more challenging. This could hinder a firm's ability to respond to economic growth, particularly in the immediate term, if the resources required are also demanded by other firms.

Technological change

The impact of technological change upon business

Technology impacts in a variety of business contexts:
- **Communication** is affected within the business, between businesses and between the business and its customers, e.g. ICT.
- **Organisational structure** is affected as employees are replaced, retrained or recruited as a result of technological change.
- **Productive technology** enables firms to lower unit costs, raise output and be more flexible in their manufacturing, e.g. CAM/CAD.
- The variety of **new products** available increases due to improvements in technology, e.g. in consumer electronics, DVDs etc.
- **Market technology** is concerned with the way businesses interact both with each other and with the consumer, e.g. the internet has created a completely new channel of distribution.

Technology might be introduced to:
(1) Gain a competitive advantage, e.g. quicker response to customers, reduced unit costs leading to lower prices.
(2) Maintain competitive position, e.g. catching up with a competitor.

Technological advantage can be copied and thus eroded. For a business to enjoy a long-term technological competitive advantage it must maintain a leading technological position. This might necessitate the constant search for new technologies.

Evaluation Whatever the reason for the introduction of a new technology, if it is to be of strategic use, it has to deliver some lasting benefit to the organisation. This benefit may only accrue in the long term once the short-term difficulties associated with change have been worked through. Further, the benefit depends upon the competitive environment and the extent to which customers perceive any additional value in the transaction with the firm.

Social factors

The role and limits of corporate responsibility

Corporate responsibility stems from the concept that businesses have their own identities. For both public and private limited companies this separate identity is legally recognised, while for non-incorporated businesses, such as sole traders and partnerships, the law makes no distinction between the business and its owner(s). If it is accepted that businesses have their own identities, their behaviour is effectively that of their employees. Hence, the business is liable for employees' acts or omissions in the course of their employment.

Corporate responsibility is important for two reasons. First, this responsibility is recognised in law through the tort of vicarious liability, which means being liable for the actions of another. Hence, a business can be sued for damages because of the actions of those it employs. Consequently, businesses need to ensure that, through their systems and procedures, their employees act in a reasonable manner at all times.

The second reason stems from the concept of being a good neighbour. Businesses are part of the community and as such their actions impinge on others. Being a nuisance neighbour will cause additional pressures for the business through complaints, protests or the intervention of the authorities, invoking regulations and the law. In either instance the business will suffer because of a reduced reputation in the market, with implications for the product it sells and/or for attracting and retaining staff.

The impact of social change

The social environment impacts upon strategic decision-making because a firm's customers are within that environment. Just as society's values evolve and develop, so too must those of a business if it is to retain credibility and relevance within its market. For example, increased public concerns about intensive farming practices have caused both producers and retailers to adopt different standards, often in advance of legislation.

The changing pattern of employment

Firms hire staff to produce output. The quantity and quality of the staff required by the business are determined in the workforce plan. Changes in the composition of the external labour market will force the firm to amend its employment practices. The composition of the labour market is changing; it is becoming increasingly part-time, flexible, educated and open to both sexes.

> **Evaluation** Social change affects businesses in a variety of ways. Moreover, social change affects the degree to which a business can secure the appropriate human resources for it to be able to deliver its strategic objectives. Increasingly, businesses seek to appear responsible by adopting 'green' policies and HRM systems to improve the welfare of employees.

The law

Legal behaviour and business decisions

The majority of law concerning business is civil law. The major areas in which the law affects businesses are:

- competition legislation, e.g. takeovers and mergers
- consumer protection, e.g. Sale of Goods Act
- employment, e.g. sex discrimination
- occupational safety, e.g. health and safety at work
- contract, e.g. delivery of raw materials

An alternative way of viewing the impact of law is to think of the various relationships a business has:

- workers, e.g. sex discrimination, health and safety at work
- suppliers, e.g. law of contract, delivery of materials
- customers, e.g. consumer protection, Sale of Goods Act
- competitors, e.g. takeovers and mergers

Contract law

A contract is an agreement that the law will recognise. Consequently, a contractual dispute between two parties, whether business to business or business to customer, can be resolved through recourse to law. The simple fact that the law provides a framework for the resolution of disputes is often enough to ensure that disputes do not arise. Hence, businesses will behave within the law because of the law. However, should a dispute arise, then it would be up to the law courts to consider the different arguments and arrive at a resolution.

Costs of litigation

Taking a dispute to the courts tends to add to the costs of a business. This need not cause an individual business competitive harm if all other businesses in the market suffer the same cost pressures. However, those competing at an international level may well find that UK and EU legalisation make them less cost competitive than businesses operating in a more laissez-faire legal environment. Such a cost disadvantage might result in lobbying of national government for protection against 'unfair' cheap imports. Alternatively, by adding additional value to the product, the business might be able to differentiate its product sufficiently from others so that customers are willing to pay a higher price, thus offsetting the cost disadvantage caused by legislation.

> **Evaluation** The impact any legislation has upon a business depends upon three main factors:
>
> (1) The extent to which the business needs to change its behaviour to comply. For example, a firm paying in excess of the National Minimum Wage (NMW) will be less affected by the NMW than one with pay levels below the minimum.

(2) The extent to which the law will be enforced. For the law to be influential the business has to believe that non-compliance will be detected. It is the role of various inspectorates, e.g. the Health and Safety Executive (HSE), to encourage compliance. A major impact of trade unions is to pressure businesses to comply or face a reduction in the quality of industrial relations.

(3) The extent to which any sanction resulting from non-compliance will cause harm to the business. Legislation that carries a small financial penalty is less likely to achieve compliance than legislation that could result in temporary or permanent closure.

Political factors

Effects of political changes and government intervention

Government is a major influence upon business strategy because of its ability to affect the operating environment. Examples of governmental influence are economic policies and the introduction of laws and regulations. In addition, government is influential because it is a major consumer, a significant employer and a provider of services, such as health and education.

Increasingly, organisations in the public sector are being encouraged to behave in a business-like, private-sector manner. Hence, schools and hospitals, while not profit motivated, nonetheless have to pay attention to delivering high levels of customer service in a cost-effective way. Consequently, although their ownership may differ, the distinction in behavioural terms between the public and private sectors is no longer as clear as before.

The establishment of regulators or 'watchdogs', e.g. OFTEL, has accompanied privatisation of major state industries, where state assets have been transferred to the private sector. It is the regulator's role to replace the working of a competitive market until such time as sufficient providers enter the industry to create genuine competition.

Deregulation of markets and industries creates opportunities for business. For example, deregulation of transport has resulted in many more bus companies.

Evaluation The extent to which private sector businesses can flourish after privatisation depends upon the nature of the privatisation itself. A regulator with the legal power to restrict strategic decisions will accompany the creation of a private-sector monopoly provider. Similarly, privatisation through operational franchise will only encourage investments that offer a return within the life of the franchise.

Environmental audits

An environmental audit is an independent assessment of the effects of a business's activities upon the physical environment. All business activity affects the physical environment. This might be in the actual provision of the good or service, e.g. energy usage and waste, as well as in the delivery of the finished item, e.g. transport congestion and disposal of packaging.

The stages in carrying out an environmental audit are:
(1) Link activity to business objectives.
(2) Decide on the aspects of activity to monitor.
(3) Decide on the criteria, e.g. levels of pollution.
(4) Create a means of recording data.
(5) Monitor the data.
(6) Control outputs to ensure compliance with criteria.

Benefits and methods of reducing process waste

Reducing the impact a business has on the physical environment does not just lead to additional costs. Internally, benefits include an improvement in employee morale. Externally, the benefits include an enhanced public profile which may lead to increased sales and advantages in recruitment.

Producing less waste might mean an improvement in efficiency, as less of the raw material that the business has purchased is discarded. This will be particularly true if the emphasis is upon the minimisation of physical waste. This can be achieved by:
(1) Not producing it in the first place!
  • improving quality, reducing rework and scrap
  • JIT, or making to order
  • improving product design
  • reducing packaging
(2) Converting the waste to a saleable by-product.
(3) Recycling.

If waste has to be produced, then the issues become:
(1) Destruction, e.g. burning/incineration.
(2) Disposal, e.g. landfill (tax).

The cost of waste management will reflect the nature of the waste being produced. In extreme cases, e.g. nuclear waste, the cost might be extremely high because, rather than disposing of the waste, the business has to store it securely.

Waste management and environmental audits are important because of the potential for negative publicity from media attention, public opinion and environmental pressure groups. Similarly, customers may have an environmental purchasing policy such that they will only buy from suppliers that have an established, ethically robust, environmental stance.

Evaluation How a business reacts to issues of physical waste management will reflect its stakeholders' views and influence. These stakeholders include employees, customers, government and owners.

Moral and ethical issues

Morals and ethics reflect values and beliefs. As such, determining a moral standpoint on an issue is highly individualistic. Being inert, businesses themselves do not have values and beliefs; rather it is the people within them who do. Hence, the moral and ethical position taken by a business reflects the values and beliefs of its stakeholders.

Modification of business behaviour

The precise position taken will arise from balancing the views of these different stakeholders and their relative influences within a specific context. For example, a shareholder who wants the business to deliver the highest possible profit at the expense of corporate responsibility to the environment would have little influence if he were a lone voice holding only a tiny fraction of the issued shares. Similarly, a business that has considerable market dominance may choose to ignore calls for a more ethically justifiable position if it feels its sales base is not threatened.

> **Evaluation** Whether an ethical position is appropriate for a business depends upon whether it assists the business in achieving its objectives. Further, a short-term cost arising from an ethical stance may deliver a longer-term advantage. It is up to the individual to weigh the circumstances and the evidence and to produce a reasoned answer rather than seeking to identify a single 'right' response.

Devising and implementing strategy

Having read the earlier section on setting corporate objectives, you should understand the essential differences between strategic and tactical decisions. In brief, strategy is concerned with how the whole organisation achieves its objective in the longer term. In contrast, tactics are concerned with individual parts of the organisation. These in turn are broken down into operational, day-to-day, decisions and actions. If the strategic objective is to be achieved, the tactical and operational actions must reflect the 'bigger picture' provided by strategy.

Communication

Communicating strategy

Senior managers may devise strategy, but everyone in the organisation delivers it. Consequently, the strategy has to be communicated throughout the organisation in such a way that everyone understands its aims and purpose and their role in its achievement. This means that communication is not merely concerned with sending messages; it is equally concerned with ensuring the message sent is the same as that received. Good communication should generate the required response, whether it is understanding the aim of the strategy or the actions required for its delivery.

The need for effective communication and consultation

Effective communication is complex because it involves people. People are different in the way in which they receive and interpret messages. These differences can create a situation whereby the message sent does not match the message received. Reasons for differences include:
- attitude, e.g. a preconceived view about a situation
- culture, e.g. a value system that influences attitudes and beliefs
- motivation, e.g. a lack of desire to hear the message
- perception, e.g. a subjective feeling that leads to distortion of the message
- physical factors, e.g. tiredness, external noise and competing messages
- prejudice, e.g. a pre-existing mindset about the person sending the message
- values, e.g. a set of ethical beliefs about the appropriateness of the message

In addition to the above, communication may be ineffective if the sender uses an inappropriate method or vocabulary.
- Methods of communication include the technical media used, e.g. visual, electronic.
- Inappropriate vocabulary includes the use of jargon or terminology with a specific specialist meaning that may not be fully understood by non-specialist staff.

One means of ensuring that the message sent is the same as that received is to build feedback into the communication process.

> **Evaluation** Effective communication depends upon the skill of the sender in using an appropriate means and vocabulary to send the message. The appropriateness of these two variables will reflect the purpose of the message, its complexity and the characteristics of the receiver. For the receiver to interpret the message sent accurately, the receiver needs to be open to the message and to trust the person sending it.

Barriers to effective communication

If the communication received differs from that sent, then it has not been effective in overcoming the barriers that surround us all. Barriers to communication take on a variety of forms and change through time and context. They include:
- **Overload**, i.e. when the receiver tries to decode too many messages at once. This may result in confusion between different messages or alternatively a feeling of not being able to cope.
- **Communication network**, i.e. the formal structure in the organisation prevents the people who need to communicate directly with each other from doing so. In this situation, the message might be distorted as it flows from the sender, through intermediaries to the receiver.

- **Remoteness from the audience**, i.e. the person sending the message lacks credibility, so the message has to overcome the barrier of the receiver's perception.
- **Attitudes**, i.e. the receiver, through past experience, has a mindset which serves to distort the message being sent, e.g. a marketing manager perceiving those within the accounts department as being dull and users of complicated, technical jargon. This immediately creates a barrier between the two departments which could reduce the effectiveness of communication within the organisation.

From corporate plan to target setting

Corporate plan

The corporate plan sets out the organisation's objectives. This plan will be both long term and organisation wide. Having set the broad aim through the corporate plan, the contribution required from each department within the organisation can be established so that there is goal congruence between departments.

Target setting

Departmental plans are detailed and short term. They become targets for those within the organisation to achieve, either at section or at individual level. For example, the corporate plan might include the objective of 4% growth in output next year. This objective means that the operations management department will have to increase output. Hence, on a quarterly and weekly basis, output must rise. The overall objective can be decomposed into a daily production target. This allows those working on the production line to know how many extra units are required each shift in order that the overall corporate plan is achieved.

Measuring effectiveness

When targets are set, those working towards them can monitor their performance and adjust it if necessary. Further, by having an objective to work towards, it becomes possible to identify those who are making the greatest contribution to the achievement of the organisation's purpose. These effective employees can then be appropriately rewarded. In contrast, those less effective employees can be offered support to help them become more effective. This might be achieved through training, for example.

Budgets

A budget is a quantified plan for some predetermined, future period of time. Budgets need not be financially based, but often are. An example of a non-financial budget would be a budget for the number of man-hours required to complete a specific activity. This hour budget can then be converted into a financial budget if the hourly labour rate is known.

Communication, control and motivation

Budgets play an important role in the effectiveness of an organisation as it works towards the achievement of its strategic objectives. This is because budgets:

- **Provide a quantifiable target**. They are short-term targets that are compatible with the longer-term strategic objectives.
- **Allocate resources**. This ensures that those who are responsible for certain actions are given the necessary resources with which to achieve them.
- **Control**. By setting a limit, a budget ensures that resources are not used unnecessarily and so wasted.
- **Identify responsibility**. By knowing who needs to do what, duplication or oversight of responsibility can be avoided. Further, through being a budget holder an individual can gain motivational responsibility.
- **Establish a means of appraisal**. After the competition of the budget period, actual and budget achievement can be compared and thus the effectiveness of the budget holder can be assessed.
- **Aid communication**. All budget holders know what their roles are within the organisation and can discuss problems and concerns with their line managers.

  Evaluation Budgets are targets for what should be achieved. Rigidly adhering to a budget in the face of internal or external change may demotivate budget holders. For budgets to be effective, budget holders have to believe they have been given a realistic target and the resources to achieve it. A budget that is imposed, rather than set through negotiation, may not meet this requirement. The effectiveness of a budget in communication, controlling and motivating rests in large part upon the skill of the budget holders and the trust between budget holders and those with whom they interact.

Adverse and positive variances

Variance is the difference between budget and actual achievement. Given the changing nature of the organisation's environment, it is almost inevitable that variances will occur. A variance is not, in itself, a sign of a problem. There are two types of variance:

- **Adverse**. This is where the difference will lead to a reduction in profit, e.g. actual revenue is lower than budgeted revenue. Alternatively, actual costs may be greater than budgeted costs.
- **Positive**. This is where the difference will lead to an increase in profit. An alternative term for a positive variance is 'favourable'. A favourable variance will arise if actual revenue exceeds budgeted revenue. Alternatively, actual costs may be lower than budgeted costs.

Calculation and interpretation of variances

A variance can be analysed into volume and value variances. If, for example, actual revenue were greater than budget, this could be for three possible reasons.

- More might have been sold. This would be a favourable volume variance.

- The selling price might have risen. This would be a favourable value variance.
- There might be some combination of both volume and value as follows:

Budgeted revenue	10,000 units @ £8 each	= £80,000
Actual revenue	12,000 units @ £7.50 each	= £90,000
Revenue variance		= £10,000 (favourable)

By analysing the £10,000 favourable variance into its value and volume components it is possible to understand it more fully. The following analytical framework makes it possible to determine the two variances.

Budgeted volume 10,000	Budgeted price £8	Budgeted revenue £80,000	Variance	
Actual volume 12,000	Budgeted price £8	Revenue £96,000	£16,000	Favourable volume variance
Actual volume 12,000	Actual price £7.50	Actual revenue £90,000	£6,000	Adverse value variance
			£10,000	Hence favourable revenue variance

Here, the value variance is adverse (£6,000), while the volume variance is favourable (£16,000): taking them together gives a favourable variance of £10,000.

From this analysis of the variance it is possible to see that the primary reason for the favourable revenue variance was a large increase in sales volumes. Indeed, had the price been maintained at the budgeted level, the overall revenue variance would have been even larger. Consequently, in assessing the performance of the budget holders, and having congratulated them for a favourable variance, one would wish to focus on why price was dropped and investigate whether this was the reason for the increase in volume. The reason for the increase in volume might have been beyond the control of the budget holders, e.g. a competitor leaving the market.

Evaluation Not all variances are necessarily a sign of effective performance. An adverse variance may be caused by factors beyond the individual's control, such as an increase in raw material costs. The value of using variance analysis, particularly as a means of assessing performance and motivating employees, depends on whether variance arises through some factor that is within the individual's control.

Management of working capital to secure liquidity

Liquidity is the immediate funding required by an organisation to meet its day-to-day obligations — its working capital. This is needed to pay wages and make payments to suppliers. A profitable business will fail if it runs out of cash with which to pay these expenses, as creditors will cease to supply the business. Thus the organisation will not achieve its objective. However, having excess cash is wasteful, as the surplus could be invested in revenue-generating activities or used to acquire other fixed assets. Wasteful use of cash, a current asset, will similarly hamper the organisation in its drive for its strategic objective.

Working capital is calculated as:

current assets – current liabilities

Two ratios assess an organisation's liquidity position:

$$\text{acid test} = \frac{\text{cash} + \text{debtors}}{\text{current liabilities}} \quad \text{(normally between 0.5 and 1.0)}$$

$$\text{current ratio} = \frac{\text{current assets}}{\text{current liabilities}} \quad \text{(normally between 1.0 and 1.5)}$$

The amount of working capital required can be estimated by calculating the business's cash cycle. This is achieved by combining three activity ratios:

	days' sales in stock	e.g. 45 days
+	days' sales in debtors	e.g. 30 days
–	creditor payment period	e.g. 60 days
=	cash cycle	e.g. 15 days

The above example suggests that the business requires sufficient working capital for 15 days of operation, i.e. the period between having to pay for raw materials and the time when customers pay for their goods. This shows that the business's liquidity requirement is closely linked to its management of working capital.

The working capital requirement can be reduced by:
- high levels of efficiency in manufacture and so low stock levels
- encouraging customers to pay cash or to settle their invoices quickly
- delaying paying creditors for the maximum time allowed

Evaluation The amount of working capital required by a business depends upon how quickly it can turn stock into sales and, in turn, how quickly it can turn sales into cash. Taking full advantage of credit offered by suppliers helps minimise the amount required. A business's ability to minimise its working capital largely reflects its bargaining position vis-à-vis its customers and suppliers. For example, although the big supermarkets receive cash from customers, they buy in such bulk from suppliers that they can demand and receive extended credit terms. The opportunity cost of working capital depends upon the level of interest rates.

The strategic importance of location

Location is one of the most strategically important decisions facing many businesses. Being in the wrong place may cause the business to have a cost disadvantage compared to competitors. For example, transport costs may be higher. Alternatively, more might have to be spent on promotion to attract trade. In each case it would mean either having to charge higher prices or accepting a lower return.

Problems with relocation

The costs involved in establishing a location can be huge, and moving location can be very expensive and disruptive. Consequently, businesses tend not to relocate unless there is an overwhelming reason to do so. Many businesses do not locate in the most cost-effective location for several reasons. These include not appreciating the cost disadvantages of a location. Similarly, stakeholders may feel comfortable with a particular location and so be reluctant to move. This is known as **inertia**.

Factors influencing location

Location is not a decision for primary sector businesses; they have to locate where the natural resource occurs.

For secondary sector businesses, a balance has to be struck between the costs of moving raw materials, the costs of processing at a particular location and the costs of transporting the finished good to the market. Processing costs would include labour costs, rents and other fixed costs.

For tertiary businesses, location is highly dependent upon the nature of the service offered. A hairdresser has to be close to its market. However, the availability of ICT means that a data-processing operation could choose to locate almost anywhere.

Financial factors

The financial costs of a particular location may well change through time. For example, wage differentials for a specific skill may increase within a country. Similarly, a multinational firm may find that taxation regimes change or that a grant initially paid is no longer available.

Non-financial factors

Whilst important, financial costs are not the only considerations in location. Non-financial factors such as the owner's objectives may play an equally important part in the decision where to locate. These non-financial factors will be most prevalent in a business with owner-managers (because of a lack of tension between these two potentially conflicting stakeholder groups). Other non-cost factors include the attitude of the local community and other stakeholders.

Problems with multi-location

Multi-location businesses face particular challenges with regard to coordination and control. For example, opening another site in the next town would place additional strains on the control and monitoring systems and procedures of a business. For these reasons a business may choose to locate at a more expensive, local, site than one that is cheaper but more remote.

Evaluation Rarely will one location be preferable to another on every criterion. Consequently, choosing a location requires decision-makers to balance the importance of different factors, both financial and non-financial. Similarly, the predictability of a location's current costs will be a factor. The location chosen will depend upon the relative importance attached to each factor by those making the decision.

Reviewing strategy

Strategy is about how organisations use their resources to achieve an objective in the context of external change. Consequently, a review of strategy is used to determine whether the objective has been achieved. A starting point in the review of strategy is the identification of the objective (see Setting corporate objectives, pages 13–16).

Market and environmental circumstances

Another aspect of strategy is to achieve competitive advantage. To monitor this the organisation will engage in a constant review of market and environmental circumstances. Some methods of analysis, such as SWOT, have already been met in the AS part of the course.

Similarly, PEST analysis can be used as a tool when reviewing the environment. The review will include an audit of the macroenvironmental factors including:
- political/legal/government
- economic
- social/cultural/demographic
- technical
- customers
- competitors
- suppliers

Evaluation Organisations operating in a relatively steady environment may not need to engage in a formal environmental review as frequently as those in a turbulent environment. Some small organisations, particularly those with a focus on short-term survival, may not engage in any form of environmental analysis and will inevitably become reactive. The success of any environmental review will reflect the expertise of those undertaking it, the resources made available and the degree to which the external dynamic situation can be predicted and understood.

Changes in market demand

Markets, because they consist of customers and competitors, are in a continual state of change. Market demand may alter due to changes in customer needs or due to a change in competitive behaviour. A review of strategy should therefore consider whether the firm's product offering is appropriate in the prevailing market conditions. Is the business producing a product which delivers customer satisfaction, while at the same time enabling it to fulfil its own objectives?

If there is a mismatch between what the firm offers and what the market requires, then the strategy being followed is inappropriate. In such circumstances the firm will need either to influence the market so its current products are once again required or else to change its products. The former might require considerable expenditure in promotion. The latter will require research and development (R&D) and new product development. By its very nature R&D is a risky activity. However, it is essential in markets subject to a lot of change, if the firm is to maintain its competitive position.

R&D and new product development

R&D and new product development broadly fall under two headings:
- **Innovation** — the development of new products. By being first into a market a firm can gain market dominance, but because this approach creates the market need it is very high risk. If a company is successful, competitors will seek to enter the market. Consequently, continual product development will be required to maintain market leadership.
- **Imitation** — launching a 'me too' product similar to a competitor's product. This is less risky but equally challenging as the business is seeking to capture sales from the innovator.

> **Evaluation** The amount of R&D required in the market will depend upon the degree of change within it. In markets with rapidly changing technologies, high levels of R&D are required to maintain market power. High levels of R&D expenditure by competitors would also encourage a similar strategy.

Financial review

Interpretation of performance through ratio analysis

A key method of assessing the achievement of objectives, as well as being a diagnostic tool in its own right, is ratio analysis. Financial ratios can be grouped into five main headings, spelling out the mnemonic SLAPS:
- **S**olvency, e.g. gearing, interest cover
- **L**iquidity, e.g. acid test, current ratio
- **A**ctivity, e.g. asset turnover, debtor turnover

- **P**rofitability, e.g. return on capital employed (ROCE), net profit margin
- **S**hareholders, e.g. earnings per share (EPS), return on equity

Appropriate calculation of ratios, being an analytical tool, will be highly rewarded in the examination. The main decision is which of the ratios to use to make sure any calculation undertaken is appropriate and thus rewardable.

Using financial accounting to assess performance

There may be a clear reason to focus on one particular aspect of the organisation's financial performance. For example, the business might be following a strategy of survival and hence the focus would be on liquidity. In such a situation the calculation of the two liquidity ratios, acid test and current ratio, would be essential. The analysis could then be broadened to consider working capital and the activity ratios concerned with cash flow, debt collection, stock turnover and creditor payments. A similar approach could be employed for other objectives, e.g. profit.

In the absence of any clear focus, the following pyramid of ratios offers a structure for interpretation.

Primary efficiency ratio

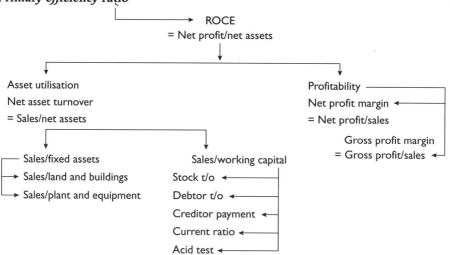

In addition, there are ratios concerned with **shareholders**: return on equity, earnings per share, dividend per share, price/earnings; and **solvency**: gearing, interest cover.

As a single ratio is based on financial information, it merely shows the organisation's performance at a particular point in time and in isolation. To be meaningful any ratio needs a comparison. This could be:
- Internal: previous years
         budget
- External: similar firms
         industry standard

Evaluation In interpreting ratios you need to think about the validity of the underlying information. For example, audited accounts can be viewed more objectively than unaudited ones. Similarly, consider the date on the accounts. The accounts of a business operating in a very seasonal market will be distorted at certain times of year: for example, a toy manufacturer would have large stocks in late summer in anticipation of orders from retailers for the Christmas market. This may make it difficult to make valid judgements. Accounts can also be subject to window dressing. The interpretation of ratios should be performed against a consideration of the business's objective and the environment in which it is operating.

The use of technology

Technology as an aid to decision-making

Managers make decisions and making decisions requires information. Technology aids decision-making through:

- storage, e.g. databases
- processing, e.g. spreadsheets
- presentation, e.g. PowerPoint
- information access, e.g. internet

Management information systems

Acquiring information communication technology (ICT) requires considerable capital expenditure. Further, staff with the appropriate skills need to be recruited or existing staff trained, thus adding to the investment required.

Technology can be regarded as the tools the business uses to perform its functions: any change in technology will have an impact on the prevailing culture. For example, widespread access to e-mail can create an impersonal culture where face-to-face communication becomes rare.

Evaluation To deliver strategic advantage the ICT systems within a business have to be appropriate for the needs of the users and deliver a benefit that exceeds their cost. A business may develop a culture of overreliance on ICT and so accept subjective information as factual. Similarly, the ease of communicating information may cause information overload.

Employee contribution to objectives

It is through employees that business strategy is delivered. Thus in reviewing strategy it is essential to be able to assess whether employees are making a positive contribution to strategy. Single measures on their own are less useful than a comparator, e.g. other firms or past internal performance. For example, an emerging downward trend in employee contribution can highlight a need for action.

For most businesses the emphasis will be upon improving employee contribution, as this lowers unit costs and so enables the firm to be more competitive.

Although numerous methods of assessment exist, the ones of greatest concern are productivity and absenteeism.

Productivity

A ratio of output to input, typically sales/employee, gives us labour productivity. The greater the value of productivity, the greater is the contribution being made. A business-wide value can disguise departmental and individual performance. Consequently, a tighter definition will lead to a more meaningful measure. But, as the measure becomes more focused on the individual level, it becomes necessary to define and measure the individual's output. In some situations, e.g. nursing, this is far from easy. Investment in technology is one method of boosting employee productivity. Others include improving working methods and staff culture.

Absenteeism

This is measured by the number of staff who miss work divided by the average number of staff employed. High levels of absenteeism indicate that the business is having to employ additional staff to cover for absences. This will increase the business's wage bill. Moreover, absenteeism is disruptive to the operation of the firm, particularly in situations where the absent individual has a unique skill or talent. Absenteeism is also a symptom of poor morale and low motivation.

> **Evaluation** To be useful, any measure of employee contribution assumes it is possible to measure an individual's output and that the individual is able to influence his or her output. A poor level of employee contribution may be symptomatic of the industry or the location of the business.

Managing strategic change

Securing resources

Financial capital is one of the key resources required by any organisation. There are two main types of capital requirement:
- **working capital** — for funding day-to-day operations
- **investment capital** — for purchasing new assets, either to expand the operation or to replace existing machinery

Securing finance for a strategic purpose, because strategy is long term, will almost inevitably require investment capital. However, the purchase of a new machine, for example, may create a need for additional working capital, e.g. a build-up of stock.

There may be an additional training requirement involved in the introduction of new technology. So, the total finance required may well be more than the purchase price of the machine.

Sources of finance

The source of finance chosen will reflect a variety of factors. These are:
- legal identity of the business, i.e. only companies can sell shares
- objectives of the owners, i.e. a desire to retain control may rule out shares
- size of the business, i.e. does it have assets for collateral?
- how soon the finance is required, i.e. urgent or later
- how much is required, i.e. proportion of existing capital structure
- how long is the finance needed for, i.e. short term or permanent
- what the finance is needed for, i.e. working capital or investment
- cost of finance, i.e. the riskier the project, the higher the cost

Sources of finance can be classified as:
- **internal** — generated from within the business by its operations
- **external** — secured from outside the business

Sources of finance

	Short term	**Medium term**	**Long term**
Internal	Retained profits Cash management Sales of surplus assets	Retained profits	Retained profits
External	Overdraft Trade credit Factoring Loan	Hire purchase Leasing Term loan	Term loan Equity Grants

Because of its long-term nature, strategic finance will usually involve either loans or equity. Raising finance from either source will have an impact upon the business's gearing ratio.

Taking on additional loans will raise the gearing ratio, reduce the interest cover ratio, and increase the risk to both equity investors and lenders. This increase in risk will be accompanied by an increase in the return required by lenders, i.e. additional finance will become more expensive to borrow.

The cost of borrowing external finance can be reduced by offering lenders worthwhile collateral, as this may be seen to reduce the risk.

> **Evaluation** There is no single correct source of finance for all eventualities. However, there are inappropriate sources of finance, such as suggesting that a small sole trader should sell shares to finance an advertising campaign. The appropriateness of the source will depend upon the situation the business is facing, which can be taken from the case study.

Incremental versus catastrophic change

How managers react to change will depend upon:
* whether the change was unexpected
* the size of the change
* the source of the change

Crisis and contingency management

Many changes can be anticipated and hence contingency plans can be drawn up in anticipation of the future change. Examples include an on-coming recession, disruption to production because of a labour dispute, and new legislation coming into force. In each situation plans can be drawn up to offset the risk posed by the anticipated change. For example, a business heavily dependent upon ICT will have a back-up facility to cover the risk of failure of its main computer system.

In very risky environments, several different contingency plans can be created to reflect the different scenarios envisaged. Such contingency plans mean the organisation is better prepared to meet the new demands brought by the changes.

Further, because the timescale is longer in contingency planning, more careful and detailed consideration can be given to the longer-term consequences of the change. Thus, for example, staff can be briefed in advance about the change; this in turn will reduce their resistance to it. It may be appropriate to rehearse some situations, particularly those of a catastrophic nature.

Types of change

Minor changes by their very nature have little long-term impact upon a business. The greater the extent of the change, and the longer the changed situation is likely to prevail, then the more adaptable the business will need to be. This may require new methods of working and changes to the size and composition of its labour force.

Internal change should be more manageable and predictable than external change. However, external change may well impact upon all firms in the industry and so pose a reduced threat to the business's competitive position in the market, e.g. the enactment of more stringent health and safety regulations.

> **Evaluation** How a business reacts to a change will depend upon the three factors listed above. The better a firm is prepared for change through continuous monitoring of its situation, the greater the chances are that it will emerge from the change in a stronger strategic position. Change need not be threatening to a firm and may in fact offer strategic advantage over less flexible and less responsive competitors.

Management of change

Any management of change requires four essential stages:

(1) **Diagnosis**, i.e. an identification and consideration of the situation.

(2) **Objective**, i.e. where do we want to be?

(3) **Prognosis**, i.e. what will happen if nothing is done?

(4) **Action**, i.e. what new action is required to reach the objective given the change?

Overcoming resistance to change

Change is often resisted by those affected by it. Consequently, a key requirement for the management of change is overcoming such resistance. This may be achieved by involving those affected by the change so that they can offer ideas and suggestions. At the very least, this approach will inform those affected about the reasons for the need to change. An understanding of the need may well reduce resistance to the change.

Organisational culture and employee participation

For such an approach to be effective there has to be a culture within the organisation of employee participation and openness. Those putting forward ideas need to believe their ideas matter and might have an impact. The extent to which this situation exists will reflect the degree to which:

- employees share the values and aims of the organisation
- the established leadership style lends itself to trust and cooperation
- past requests for participation have been effective
- channels of communication are open and clear
- the change brings opportunities for employee development
- the change threatens established working practices, groups and routines

Once the need for change has been established and subsequently agreed, the task is to implement the change. The method by which it is carried out will reflect the culture within the organisation and the urgency of the need for change. A 'macho' management culture, Taylorite in attitude to the employees, is unlikely to be successful in winning over employees to the need for change and the company's response to it.

Employee relations at individual and collective level

Change impacts both upon individuals in the workforce and upon the whole workforce as a collective body. To effect change therefore requires good relations at both the individual and the collective level. At the collective level this could mean collective bargaining, whereby the employer negotiates with a representative body of the employees rather than with individuals.

Evaluation The ability of management to motivate and effect change will largely depend upon the extent to which employees recognise the need for change and their trust in the managers to implement the appropriate response for the benefit of all stakeholder groups, not least of which will be the employees themselves. Unless the nature of the change is catastrophic and unexpected, such a situation will only prevail within a culture of shared values and mutual respect.

Trade unions

Trade unions exist to improve their members' employment terms and conditions. Their ability to influence employers to change their behaviour in favour of employees depends upon their power. A trade union's power is greatest when:
- there is a high level of union membership
- those seeking influence have an essential role in the firm's revenue creation, such that any disruption will be immediately apparent
- the firm is enjoying a period of good sales, with high orders and low stocks
- public opinion is sympathetic to their cause
- the skills possessed by the employees are in scarce supply
- management wishes to have a long-term relationship with the trade union

Their role in achieving corporate objectives

In representing their members, trade unions have similar long-term objectives for the business to many other stakeholder groups, namely stability and prosperity. A dispute that results in a short-term gain for either the employees or employers at the expense of the other may well be counterproductive in the long term. Consequently, a trade union can play an essential role in delivering long-term business success if it forces the employer to focus on the needs of other stakeholders.

Their role in changing employment practices and levels

There are likely to be times when the aims of employees and employers are different and disputes will arise. This may mean that trade unions obstruct employers in their immediate plans for the business. Traditionally, trade unions have been viewed as seeking only to maximise the pay, conditions and employment levels of the employees and therefore as a hindrance to employers, acting to obstruct and frustrate the management and hence the direction of the business.

Evaluation Trade unions, in representing the employees, can articulate the aims and concerns of the employees far more effectively than employees could individually. Further, if through discussions with employers trade unions recognise the need for change, they can express that need to the employees. Employees, hearing of the need for change from their representatives, are likely to be less hostile to the message than if that same message had come directly from their employer. As such, the role of trade unions in relation to corporate objectives is not solely negative.

Flexible working

Flexible working practices enable the business to be more responsive to market changes and as such it is more likely to enjoy a strategic advantage. By being able to use employees flexibly, the business can more closely match its wage cost structure to its revenue creation.

Flexible working practices

There are a wide variety of flexible working practices, including:
- multi-skilled employees
- removal of job demarcation
- annualised hours contracts
- split-shift working
- increasing the proportion of part-time staff in the workforce
- zero-hour contracts
- sub-contracting
- core and peripheral workers

Flexible working can mean the reduction of job and income security for employees. As such it is often resisted or accepted only with reluctance. Those with few skills, or non-transferable skills, may have little choice other than to accept. This is particularly the case when one employer dominates an industry, e.g. postal services.

> **Evaluation** The ability of employers to enforce flexible employment practices will depend upon the conditions in the labour market, both local and national. Those employees with few alternative job opportunities may accept the imposition of changed working routines. Given an upturn in their employment prospects elsewhere, they may then leave for a more secure environment. However, if the benefits of flexible working practices are shared, they are more likely to be accepted and viewed positively.

Strategies for avoiding conflict

In negotiations with employers about pay, working conditions and employment practices, employees, through their trade union or other representative body, will seek to influence the employer. Where the two parties cannot agree, a conflict will emerge. The employees may, as part of their attempt to resolve the conflict in their favour, threaten or actually take industrial action.

Forms of industrial action include:
- working to rule
- overtime bans
- go slows
- strikes, i.e. the withdrawal of labour

content guidance

Industrial action is disruptive. It has a cost for both employees, in terms of lost wages, and employers, in terms of lost output. Increasingly, employers and employees are establishing mechanisms to avoid the need for industrial action as outlined below.

No-strike deals

A binding agreement that employees will continue to work whilst negotiating. The forming of a no-strike deal would typically be accompanied by some concession to employees from the employer.

Pendulum arbitration

Agreeing that the dispute will be settled by the acceptance of either the employees' demands or the employer's offer. No middle ground, no compromise, is acceptable — an outside arbitrator decides which of the two alternatives will be adopted. This has the effect of reducing the extremity of the positions taken at the start by both parties and so reduces the distance between them in negotiations.

The role of intermediaries

If a dispute arises, a neutral third party, typically an industrial relations expert, may be used. The intermediary's role may be binding or advisory. In the former case the intermediary listens to the arguments put forward by both sides, weighs the evidence and then comes to a decision that the parties have agreed in advance to accept. If the intermediary is acting in an advisory role, he or she can only mediate and facilitate the discussion towards a decision, but not make it on behalf of the two parties.

Advisory Conciliation and Arbitration Service (ACAS)

This is a body established by government to promote good industrial relations. ACAS can act as a neutral intermediary in cases of dispute. However, it can also advise both parties during negotiations so that a dispute becomes less likely. Another important part of the role of ACAS is that of offering employers and employees advice on good industrial relations practice, e.g. disciplinary and grievance procedures, such that disputes are less likely to occur.

> **Evaluation** The success of any strategy in resolving a dispute will depend upon the two parties' commitment to a long-term, mutually beneficial relationship. A multinational company that is able to switch its production around the globe may feel little commitment to promoting good industrial relations within a country. In contrast, an employer committed to an area and employing highly skilled and marketable employees will be more willing to devise strategies that minimise the risk of harmful industrial relations disputes.

Questions
&
Answers

In this section of the guide there are two case study questions. The case studies are pre-issued, but the questions are seen for the first time in the examination. This means that the approach adopted for the AS Module 2873, Business Behaviour, is appropriate for this examination. The cases in this guide are followed by typical examination questions and two sample answers.

The case studies and questions follow the format of the A2 specification and specimen papers. After each case there are four questions.

Each of the four questions requires an evaluative approach for top marks to be awarded. This can be shown by considering the way the marks for each question are allocated for the four different levels of response.

Question	L1	L2	L3	L4	Total
Q1	3	4	5	6	18
Q2	4	4	5	6	19
Q3	4	4	5	6	19
Q4	3	5	6	6	20
Total	14	17	21	24	76
QWC*					4
Paper total					80
*QWC = quality of written communication					

As was stated in the Introduction, you should be aiming to work at a pace of about 1½ minutes per mark. It should be possible to write a full, evaluative answer to each of the four questions in just under 30 minutes.

Ideally you should attempt the questions in the guide (in the time allowed) before you read the sample answers. You are not expected to achieve perfection to gain an A grade — all you have to do is gain enough marks! The total number of marks for an A grade can be gained in a variety of ways. As a general guide, an A grade will be awarded to a script in which all the answers contain good analysis and some contain sound evaluation. In contrast, a C grade will be awarded to a script in which all the answers contain good application and some contain sound analysis.

You will find examiner comments on both the student answers for each case study. These comments are preceded by the icon ℯ. They are intended to point out pitfalls and common errors, and to show relatively easy ways of improving your answer and gaining marks. Making the best use of your knowledge through strong examination technique and answer strategy really can lift a performance by a grade or more.

Nuneton Nursery

Every cloud has a silver lining according to Lesley Cowley. It seems that every time she meets a crisis, a solution materialises which offers great potential. She and her mother, Susan, own Nuneton Nursery, a daycare facility catering for the under 5s.

Shortly after the birth of her son Christopher, Lesley tried to return to full-time work. She soon discovered that the provision of daycare for the under 5s in Upham was totally inadequate and she was unable to secure a place for Christopher at a council-run nursery. In the absence of any suitable local provision, she felt there were only two realistic choices. First, she could take an extended career break until Christopher was of school age. Alternatively she could move from Upham to be closer to her mother in Nuneton. This she did. By doing this she thought that she would be able to get a job whilst her mother looked after Christopher during the day. However, moving towns meant having to change jobs, and finding a new job proved far from easy. Hence it was as much by circumstance as design that Lesley ended up enrolling on a 2-year, full-time, training course with a view to becoming a qualified nursery nurse.

Having gained an NNEB (Nursery Nurse Examination Board) qualification, Lesley registered with the local authority. After a few minor alterations to the ground floor of Susan's three-storey Edwardian house, Lesley set herself up in business using the name Nuneton Nursery. However, although Susan's house provides the location, and she has considerable capital invested in the business, she takes no part in its running. As Christopher was just over 3 years old when the nursery was set up, Lesley was immediately able to accept three other children of the same age whilst remaining within the council's staff:child ratio guideline of 1:8 for 3–5 year olds. **Table 1** details the council guideline ratios for staff:child as well as child:space in square metres. Given Lesley's dedication, training and caring manner, it was no surprise that the business flourished and numbers increased.

Table 1

Age of children	Staff : child ratio	Child : space ratio (m^2)
under 2 years	1:3	1:4.0
2 years old	1:4	1:3.3
3–5 years	1:8	1:3.0

Some time later Lesley and Susan requested permission from the council for expansion of numbers. The expansion required the conversion of the entire ground floor of the house. This, and their big garden, became the designated nursery. Each of the other two floors is a self-contained flat. Before permission was granted they were visited by various agencies including social services, health and safety, fire and planning to ensure that the myriad regulations would be complied with. The provision of childcare is highly regulated and strict legal requirements exist, the principal legislation being the Children Act 1989. However, in common with all businesses, the nursery must comply with other legislation. All of the visitors proved to be enthusiastic and gave the pair very useful advice. Consequently Lesley approached Susan's bank manager with a well-researched business plan showing the required capital injection. The plan included detailed cash flow projections and clearly demonstrated the viability of the scheme. Susan offered her house as security for the loan.

Nuneton Nursery is currently registered for up to 26 children and it has a total of nine full-time equivalent employees. All care staff are required to possess a suitable accredited qualification. The average wage is £750 per month. The nursery is divided into four main areas, in addition to a kitchen and cloakroom built onto the rear of the house. One area is dedicated for the 0–2 year olds, another for the 2–3s whilst the third is for the 3–5s. The fourth area is used as a reception area for parents to drop off and collect their children. The garden is used by all of the groups and it contains a wide range of equipment. For example, it has a coverable sand pit, a water area that can be drained every night, swings, climbing frames and a Wendy house. In addition it has a large open space that permits the children to run about, 'gaining gross motor skills' as a council inspector once termed it.

The expansion has not been without problems, however. Soon after the expansion was completed Lesley agreed with a local firm of solicitors to guarantee the provision of up to five nursery places for its staff in return for a small monthly fee. Recently Lesley has been advised by the firm, Woods and Walker, of its intention to exercise its option for the first time in over 2 years. A clerk will be returning from maternity leave in 2 months' time. The arrangement allows the firm access to nursery facilities without actually having to provide these itself. The agreement suited Lesley as it provided an inflow of funds whilst the nursery was still expanding. However, as the nursery now has a waiting list for all age groups, Lesley feels that it no longer needs the fee. Another problem is friction which arises between the nursery's next-door neighbours and the parents because of parking difficulties. Noise is also an occasional irritant. A further problem is Lesley's disappointment in having to turn away requests for admission as she fully understands parents' reliance on scarce, quality, care places. She enjoys running the nursery and is anxious that it is accessible to as many families as possible. Whilst profit is a consideration, Lesley is equally concerned for the welfare of the children in her charge.

To overcome the capacity problems, Christine Lee, an employee and good friend of Lesley, has suggested further expansion. Christine has indicated that she and her husband would be willing to inject a substantial amount of capital into the business. This would fund the expansion without recourse to significantly more borrowing. In return for the capital, the Lees want part-ownership. A few years ago Christine's nephew investigated demand for nursery places as part of his A-level business studies coursework. The extracts from his assignment, shown in **Appendices 1–4**, are secondary data. Lesley has found some of these extracts interesting and they tend to confirm her own experience. Lesley also believes the demand for childcare is income-elastic. Demography influences demand as well, as do divorce rates. During the 1980s there were an average of 105,000 divorces per year involving couples with more than one child. Whilst demand for childcare in Nuneton outstrips supply, competition does exist, mainly from the parents' unpaid family and friends. Amongst some sections of the community, principally socioeconomic groups A and B, the support provided by the family tends to be replaced by nannies or au pairs. Lesley feels that, as even small children benefit from the social interaction provided in a nursery environment, the business has a significant competitive advantage over these other forms of childcare.

Two possible expansion sites are under consideration. One option is to purchase the adjacent house, which has recently come onto the market at an asking price of £215,000. With some minor building work and slight alterations, the property could take up to 30 children. The actual number would depend upon the ages of the children (see **Table 1**).

The other option is to lease an industrial unit on the town's trading estate. A 1,000 square metre unit is available with a 5-year lease for an annual rent of £45 per square metre. Rent is payable each quarter in advance. An architect friend has indicated that the unit has the potential for conversion into a nursery. The unit's hard-standing loading area is bounded by a secure fence and could readily be resurfaced as a play area. Installation of partitions and a suspended ceiling would enable the large open space to be broken down into more suitably sized areas.

Before Lesley makes any decision, she intends to use the business's computer to model possible scenarios. This will enable her to assess how sensitive the two proposals are to change in a number of variables. The most significant variable is the number of children on roll, which directly affects revenue. The nursery has a pricing policy of charging the same fee for each age group. Currently the monthly fee is £500. Lesley tries to ensure fees are paid 1 month in advance, although bad debts do arise occasionally. The roll also affects many of the business's direct costs, notably nappies and feeding. Lesley budgets direct monthly costs as £80, £60 and £50 for the 0–2s, 2s and 3–5s respectively. Another way numbers impact is via the council's staff:child ratio. This requirement means that the nursery's total cost curve is stepped and its marginal cost curve has a spiked shape. Lesley is required by the local authority to keep information on each child, for example date of birth (DOB), doctor's name, parent/carer contact, ethnic group etc. She uses a computer database to fulfil this requirement. An abridged print-out of the current roll is shown in **Appendix 5**.

With possible expansion in mind, Lesley is particularly interested in the market research conducted by Christine's nephew. The reported methodology is a random sample totalling 86 women interviewed face to face on Nuneton's high street on two consecutive Wednesday afternoons. Although Lesley recognises that the data are now 2 years old, she nevertheless thinks they contain some useful information. Combining the market research and her own experience, she feels that there might well be demand for an additional nursery. The number of children expected to attend the nursery, if the trading estate option is taken, is shown in **Table 2**. Lesley assumes that rent and fees would be paid on the first of each month.

Table 2

| Month | Attendance according to age group (forecast) | | | |
	Children under 2 years	Children 2 years old	Children 3–5 years	Total all ages
January	6	8	8	22
February	6	12	16	34
March	9	12	16	37

Expected monthly indirect costs are £2,500. Prior to opening, Lesley would purchase 2 months of stock based on the figures for January. The monthly purchases after the first month would be the stock used in the preceding month. She feels that this is enough information for her to be able to draw up some possible budgeted figures.

Appendix 1 Source of under-5 childcare according to mother's economic status*

| Source of under-5 childcare | Economic status of mother | | | | |
	Mothers in full-time employment (%)	Mothers in part-time employment (%)	Mothers currently unemployed (%)	Mothers not active economically (%)	% of total
School nursery	29	35	19	19	25
Unpaid family/ friends	36	38	19	15	24
Private scheme	11	20	16	17	17
Childminder	38	15	3	2	11
Council nursery	3	7	3	8	7
Employer	3	1	–	–	1

*Columns may sum to more than 100% as more than one source may be used.

Appendix 2 Total weekly cost (£) of under-5 childcare according to mother's economic status

| Economic status of mother | Total weekly cost of childcare (£) | | | | | |
	No cost	0.01–5.00	5.01–10.00	10.01–20.00	20.01–40.00	> 40.00
In full-time work (%)	30	8	5	9	19	29
In part-time work (%)	41	26	13	7	9	4
Not working (%)	43	38	11	5	2	1

Appendix 3 Number of live births per year according to age of mother

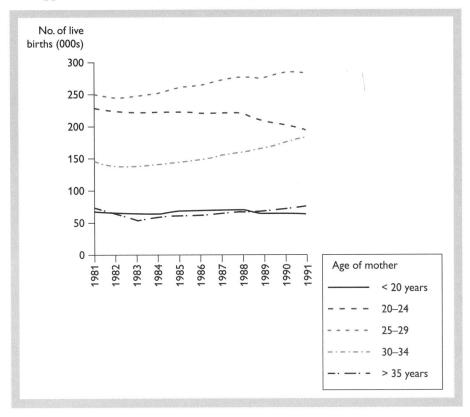

***Appendix 4 Under-5 age distribution, actual and projected,
in England and Wales (thousands)***

1971	3,951
1976	3,226
1981	3,006
1986	3,183
1989	3,346
1991	3,450
1996	3,656
2001	3,512
2011	3,205
2021	3,452
2031	3,375

Source: Annual Abstract of Statistics

Appendix 5 Nuneton Nursery, child roll current at 1/11/01

Surname	First name	DOB	Fees paid to
Balenda	Anjella	11/1/01	31/12/01
Bhatt	Prashant	4/6/97	30/11/01
Butler	Jane	31/8/00	31/12/01
Christodolou	Sohia	3/6/00	31/10/01
Clarke	Jennifer	25/11/00	31/12/01
Georgiou	Demitri	26/8/01	30/11/01
Gibbins	Christopher	15/8/99	30/11/01
Goldberg	Daniel	3/5/00	30/10/01
Hayashi	Yuri	27/7/00	31/9/01
Hershman	Michael	6/10/99	31/10/01
Jackson	Michael	23/4/99	31/12/01
Jackson	Julia	23/4/99	31/12/01
Jones	Timothy	8/7/99	30/11/01
Keown	Julian	7/7/97	30/11/01
Lee	Robert	22/3/99	31/12/01
Ma	Alvin	17/10/97	31/12/01
Mager	Robert	18/5/98	31/1/01
Martin	Elizabeth	9/10/00	31/12/01
Morris	David	25/1/99	31/12/01
Patel	Pritesh	8/12/96	31/10/01
Patel	Minesh	12/7/97	30/11/01
Shih	Yu	16/2/99	31/12/01
Ward	Thomas	14/2/01	31/8/01
Ward	Emily	30/6/98	31/8/01
Williams	Sara	12/11/00	31/12/01
Yoshida	Asuka	24/12/99	31/11/01

Answer all questions

(1) Evaluate the role budgeting can play in implementing strategy within
Nuneton Nursery.   (18 marks)

(2) Critically assess how changes in the external environment might affect the
strategic management of Nuneton Nursery.   (19 marks)

(3) Discuss the strategic implications of expansion for Nuneton Nursery.   (19 marks)

(4) Discuss how differing stakeholder objectives might influence the firm's
behaviour in the light of the notice it has received from Woods and Walker.   (20 marks)

Total: 76 marks

Answer to case study 1: candidate A

(1) All businesses need resources and Nuneton Nursery is no different. For example, in running the business Lesley needs capital and employees, both of which are resources. Acquiring these is expensive and increases the costs of the business. Although profit is not Lesley's main aim, it is nonetheless important because if the business does not at least break even, it will fail. So Lesley needs to have enough resources to run the business efficiently, but not too many so they are being wasted. She needs to strike a balance between not having enough capital which would hinder the operation of the business and having too much which would unnecessarily increase the interest charges on this borrowing.

🗭 This is not a good start. The key specification term in the question, 'budgeting', does not even get a mention in this opening paragraph.

By drawing up a budget, Lesley can see how much of each type of resource she needs. Although a budget is usually in amounts of money, it need not be. So, a budget can be used to see how much labour is needed. Table 1 shows how the number of staff changes with the number of children and their ages. So, if Lesley decided to expand the nursery by opening on the trading estate, she can use this information to budget how many staff she will need by using Table 2. In January she will need 6/3 + 8/4 + 8/8 which is five staff. So her wage bill would be 5 × £750 = £3,750, giving her a profit of £7,250. In February, 8 staff are needed (8/3 + 12/4 + 16/8), but the extra child in March has no impact on the staff needed (9/3 + 12/4 + 16/8). So Lesley can use a workforce budget to hire the right number of staff at the right time. By using a budget she knows that 5 staff are enough for January, but by February she will have to hire 3 more, which will then be enough for March. By hiring enough staff she can ensure she doesn't pay out unnecessary costs of wages or recruitment before the staff are actually needed.

🗭 Rather than discuss budgets in the way set out in the specification (communication, control and motivation), the candidate has sought to analyse the case material to show how a budget can be used for resourcing. This explicit lack of focus is a disappointment but one that does not prevent the bulk of the marks being awarded. The determination of the number of employees required is acceptable if the candidate is given the benefit of the doubt that workforce planning is analogous to budgeting. By engaging in quantitative analysis of the case data, and by bringing two different pieces of evidence together, the candidate has done enough to convince the reader to award L3.

The business can also use a budget to see how much capital it needs. Again, looking at the expansion to the trading estate it can be worked out how much working capital is needed. I have previously worked out that the business needs £20,220 in January, £9,860 in February and £10,460 in March. So, by budgeting, Lesley is able to go to the bank and arrange to have this money in advance. If she didn't have enough money, then the operation of the nursery might suffer. For example, they might run out of nappies, which would mean the parents of the children would be unhappy because of the poor quality of the childcare. At the moment Lesley enjoys a good reputation for her quality that she would be keen to keep. A lack of capital may tarnish this reputation and so lose customers. If this happens, then she might have to advertise or use other methods of marketing to get customers back, which would mean her costs would increase.

> ✐ This paragraph illustrates a weakness seen in many responses to pre-issued case studies. Although the candidate has achieved a working capital requirement, he has not explained his method or thought processes. Unless the values quoted are those expected, then the skill being exhibited is L2, the application of case material. However, the main benefit of the paragraph is the attempt to think integratively: the candidate has moved from a financial consideration into recognising potential operations and marketing issues. This is encouraging and reflects the clear specification requirement to see business studies as a whole subject rather than a series of discrete behaviours. The final paragraph reinforces this good point.

So, it is better to budget to estimate the business's resource needs because a lack of resources will be felt throughout the business. This is especially the case in this business because it is a nursery and parents will want the best for their children, and so Lesley cannot afford to let quality slip because she hasn't budgeted properly. By budgeting she can ensure she controls the resources she needs to run the business.

> ✐ Regrettably the answer does not contain evaluation. This might have been possible by, for example, balancing the costs and benefits of recruiting additional staff before the projected market demand suggests they are needed.

(2) Strategic management is concerned with how the business secures, coordinates and controls resources to achieve the objective within the constraints of external influences. External influences may offer the business opportunities for progress. Conversely they might act as limitations upon the way the business behaves, in which case the business has to adapt so that it can continue to be successful. The major influences in the business's external environment can be described using PEST: Political, Economic, Social, Technical.

> ✐ This is a good start. It demonstrates that the candidate has read and understood the question and sets the scene for the rest of the answer.

For Nuneton Nursery, one of the major political influences is through law. That the business has to comply with space and staffing ratios, which in turn depend upon the age of the child, are clear examples. Hence, if the law changed so that the child staff ratio fell, then the business would have no option but to comply with the law. This means that either more staff would need to be hired or that the number of children accepted into the nursery would have to fall. In either case the impact would be to raise the labour cost of caring for each child. Unless Lesley is willing to absorb this additional cost and accept a lower profit, the fees charged would have to rise. Although this may not appear to be attractive from a marketing point of view, it would be all right because all of the other nurseries would also be raising their fees in order to comply with the same law. The scope for achieving a competitive advantage in the face of restrictive legislation is very limited. This is because it is not possible to get staff to be more efficient as a means of reducing labour cost due to the child:staff ratio.

In this paragraph the candidate brings his understanding of the subject to the situation. The discussion shows an appreciation of the impact the law might have in this context. The fact that the business would not necessarily suffer because of a change in the law is clearly reasoned and so the judgement made is fully supported — this is enough to gain L4. Had there been a greater recognition of the need to consider strategic management, further marks could well have been achieved. It is a pity that, having set out what strategic management is in the first paragraph, this wasn't revisited and exemplified in the context of changing legislation.

The extent to which competitive advantage can arise from changes in the economic environment is similarly limited. The case shows that there is a correlation between mothers' occupation and willingness to use childcare. But, there is little that the business can do about levels of economic activity; rather it would be reactive to local changes in the labour market. However, the business could extend the idea of offering childcare facilities to local businesses or setting up near to other business to reduce the difficulties mothers may have of getting their child to the nursery. In being mainly reactive the business would need to adapt in the face of changed economic conditions. For example, during a recession the nursery would find demand falling as unemployment rose. This would in turn lower the need for staff and, if demand fell enough, Lesley may have to lay staff off. Depending upon how long they have worked for Lesley, they may be entitled to redundancy pay, which would temporarily increase the costs of the business at the very time when income is falling. But demand would have to fall a long way as the business has a waiting list.

Changes in the social environment would be numerous. For example, it could include social attitudes to childcare, birth rates, divorce rates and so on. How the management of the business changes would depend upon the local conditions and the nature of the change. Similarly the technological environment offers both opportunities and threats for the management of the business. For example, the availability of cheap PCs means Lesley can store client and child information on a database. This would be very useful in case of emergency, or in trying to arrange children into groups in, for example, target marketing. But introducing technology like this would mean capital cost of the machine and training costs for whoever operates it.

The candidate's use of PEST as the skeleton for his answer helps to ensure there are no major omissions. Two elements of PEST, economic and social, are well developed in these paragraphs, indicating that the candidate has recognised the need to be aware of skills as much as content.

Overall, the effect of the external environment on the strategic management of the nursery will depend upon a number of factors. First, the nature of the change as discussed. Second, the extent of the change — whether it is a small or larger event. Third, whether the change was anticipated so that managerial steps were already being taken.

> *This paragraph neatly rounds off a generally good answer. One concern beginning to emerge is the length of the answers given. While full answers should be given, it is also important that each of the four questions is allocated sufficient time. Whether this concern is justified remains to be seen.*

(3) The decision whether or not to expand a business is a major one which has to be thought about carefully. Although it is possible for many businesses to expand output for short periods of time by working overtime or subcontracting, these possibilities are not feasible here. Because the nursery is targeting working mothers, they will only want to use the nursery when they are at work. Having the nursery open for longer hours is unlikely to attract new business into the nursery and so profits would fall rather than rise. This is because no new customers would be attracted so revenue would stay the same, but the staff would certainly want overtime and so the wage bill would rise. Lesley could subcontract, but there are big risks doing this because of quality.

> *This opening paragraph clearly sets out the case for expansion by arguing that short-term solutions for overcapacity working are inappropriate in this context.*

To serve more customers, the business has to expand. There are several implications of this decision, which I assume she will think about. First, expanding will cause the costs of the business to rise. The extra children will cover the variable costs and if there are no extra children, then these costs — nappies and food — will disappear. However, the fixed costs won't. Fixed costs are costs that do not change with output, for example rent. So, before expanding, one implication is that the business might lose profit if it can't attract enough new customers. In the case we are told that demand exceeds supply and that the nursery has a waiting list that means there will be enough new customers. But in years to come birth rates may fall and then there won't be, so the implication is that the survival of the business becomes much more vulnerable to changes in demand because of the increase in fixed costs.

> *The good start is consolidated in this second paragraph through the recognition of the risks associated with a strategic decision to expand. Here, one implication is identified — that of market demand.*

Another implication is that Lesley will need to find more staff because of the legal restrictions on the number of children to staff. This means she will have to recruit more trained people. At the moment she employs at least nine staff all at the same place. If she expands, the communication with her staff will become more difficult because there will be more of them and some of them might be at a different site.

This will make controlling and coordinating staff much more difficult. The risk is that with more staff it will be difficult for Lesley to interact with all of them and so a feeling of alienation and remoteness might arise. They might feel that because they don't see Lesley as much, she doesn't care any more and hence they might think 'why should we', so increasing alienation. This is a major problem for the business because it is a service provider. The consumer, the child, is in direct and lengthy contact with the staff who, if they do not share the values of the business, may tell the customer, the mother, that they aren't happy. This would lead to a loss of customers for the business. So, growth has the strategic implication of communication and control between Lesley and her larger workforce.

e This paragraph explores in some depth the consequences of increasing the size of the workforce. The linkage to communication and morale is well made. Moreover, the candidate is at pains to make sure his answer is relevant to the type of business in the case study. This is apparent in the linkage between alienation and quality within an environment in which consumer satisfaction would be paramount. An interesting point is the candidate's use of the terms 'consumer' and 'customer'. It is assumed that this is deliberate, serving to enhance the quality of the answer.

Similarly, if the business expands to the industrial estate, Lesley will have to appoint a manager to control this site whilst she works at the house. This will be a hard decision for Lesley because up to now it has been her who has run the business (her mother doesn't interfere). Appointing a manager (maybe her mother or possibly Christine who wants to share in the business) will mean she will have to trust someone with her business. This is a common situation for small businesses that grow. With another manager comes a second level of hierarchy, with a tendency for slower and distorted communication. But in a relatively small business this second level of hierarchy is unlikely to be a major problem, whereas coordination across two sites might well be.

e This paragraph develops the implications of expansion further through discussing organisational structure and managerial roles. The candidate is evaluating by seeking to see both sides of the situation.

To overcome these implications, Lesley might have to formalise her business and hold meetings with staff. She will have to use more formal communication methods and use informal methods less. The aim has to be to continue to utilise the resources available to her, her staff, in the best way that still enables her to reach the objective of the business. The implication of this is that Lesley will have to spend more of her time being a manager and less and less being a nursery school teacher.

e The final paragraph is an attempt to conclude the answer and to bring it back to the question. As a conclusion it is not especially strong because the linkage back to strategy is not developed fully. However, the answer would have been less impressive had it not been there. Overall, this is another very good answer that would gain access to the highest level by virtue of the skills displayed within it.

(4) In common with all businesses, the nursery has a number of different stakeholders. These include Lesley herself as owner, her customers, her neighbours and her staff. Each group will have their own particular interest in the business and will seek to influence the business accordingly. For example, the neighbours will want a quiet life and so will try to get the business to reduce the noise it causes — a social cost.

The notice from Woods and Walker causes Lesley a problem on two levels. There is an immediate problem that the nursery appears full, from Appendix 5. However, Lesley is lucky in that she has two months' warning. Analysis of Appendix 5 shows that by this time the eldest child, Pritesh Patel, will be leaving. This means she will have a space and so can take the child. This is what Woods and Walker expect and so they would have no reason to cause problems for Lesley. Their objective will be to be treated in accordance with their contract, something which Lesley can do without changing the behaviour of the business.

> Although the opening paragraph is good, the second is better. Recognising that the problem is complex is good — few business problems are straightforward. The candidate's reasoning about the immediacy of the problem cannot be faulted — as it arises from analysis of the evidence, this means that half of the marks could be awarded.

On another level there is the risk that Lesley has already promised the next place to another customer. This customer may well get angry that another child appears to have queue jumped. Depending upon what Lesley may have promised, the customer may feel so let down that they damage the reputation of the business. Although in the short term this may not appear to be an issue (because of the long waiting list), no business can afford to alienate its customers. This is especially so in a business such as child care where a lot of business will be generated by word-of-mouth. Just like Woods and Walker, this customer will want to be treated fairly, something the business seems unable to do because of its capacity problems. If one of Lesley's objectives for the business is ethical treatment of customers, then the notice may act as a spur towards the expansion already being considered.

> Although speculative, this discussion of possible consequences is good.

In the longer term Lesley has to decide whether she wants to carry on with the agreement with Woods and Walker. When the business was getting going it was beneficial. However, as Lesley no longer needs it as badly, she might think about cancelling it. If she does this, she will have to be careful because they are solicitors and so will know their legal rights!

Before deciding how the firm deals with the notice, Lesley will have to analyse carefully the influence of the different stakeholders. The behaviour of the business will ultimately reflect the combined influence of the stakeholders, always remembering that as owner Lesley's objectives will play a key role in deciding what to do.

✐ The attempt to develop a strategic approach is good. It is entirely correct that Lesley may well have to undertake another stakeholder analysis before she redefines the business's direction and hence behaviour. As before, the candidate has sought to use the case material sensibly, demonstrating that he is familiar with all of the evidence and can select from it appropriately. This would enable him to access the higher reaches of the mark range with comparative ease.

One weakness of the answer is that it contains little that links stakeholders' objectives and the behaviour of the firm. Rather, it appears that the candidate has answered the question 'How should Lesley react to Woods and Walker?' — possibly this is a question that the candidate anticipated. However, the fact that the candidate recognises the link between a possible ethical objective and expansion means he would be awarded at L4.

✐ **Overall, the candidate would gain a grade A. The answers are consistently good given the pressures of the examination. Remember, the examiner recognises these pressures and so does not seek perfection. Answers that are relevant and consistently demonstrate the higher-order skills will secure a top grade.**

■ ■ ■

Answer to case study 1: candidate B

(1) A budget is a plan of what the business thinks will happen in the future. Setting budgets can help the business with future planning because it gives them something to aim for. By having an aim they can tell how well they are doing by comparing what they said would happen in the budget with what actually did happen. This means the business can check its progress as it goes along. If they find that there is a big difference between the two, then the managers can take steps to correct the business so that they get back on track so that it can reach its goal at the end of the budget.

✐ This opening paragraph correctly focuses upon a key aspect of the specification, budgets, but does not relate it to the question. Moreover, the use of the term 'managers' suggests a lack of appreciation of the context. Lesley wholly manages the nursery, Susan's role being that of a silent partner. Hence, the pluralisation of manager is inappropriate.

Budgets are also good for communicating because they can be used to tell the people in the business what they need to do and when they need to do it. This means that everybody in the business knows what is going on and how what they do fits into the whole business. This will make them more involved and increase their motivation, as Mayo said, because they feel part of the team. By being more motivated, the people will be more productive and efficient and so the business will be run better and profits will rise. This is good for Nuneton Nursery because the business aims to make a profit.

This paragraph continues to focus on budgets, but again bears little relevance to the question set or the context of the case study. For example, it states that the business is profit driven when we are clearly told in the case that profit 'is a consideration', not the overriding aim.

Also by having a budget the managers can tell which are their good workers and which ones aren't. A good worker will stick to their budget and not spend all of the company's money which would mean profits would fall. A good worker can then be promoted up the business which will motivate them because it moves them up Maslow's pyramid and gives them recognition which Hertzberg said is a motivator.

Here the business is described as a company even though there is no evidence in the case to support this view. Indeed, given that the title of the case makes no reference to a company, there is a stronger argument for thinking the business is in fact a partnership.

Budgets are best when the managers sit down with the worker and agree the budget. If the manager tells the worker what the budget is, then the worker will think it is unfair and so not work hard to do what the budget says. So it is best if the worker is involved in setting the budget because this means they will feel more involved. If the workers feel the budget is theirs, they will work harder to try to stick to it because they will feel responsible. The only problem is that all this will take time and when the manager is with the workers they are not doing the other things they should, so that is a disadvantage.

In evaluation I think that budgets will help the business secure resources because there are more advantages than disadvantages and so Lesley should use budgets.

This is not a particularly good answer. There are several quite serious weaknesses in it that mean that it would score less than half marks. One such weakness is the tangential nature of the answer. With the exception of the final paragraph, there is no explicit consideration of strategy within the context of the case study. Even though the final paragraph makes some reference to the context, this is not particularly strong. Rather, it seems that the candidate has merely remembered to reread the question and has noticed the need to write about Nuneton Nursery.

The answer as a whole suffers from a lack of evaluation or analysis. Although the final paragraph professes to be evaluation, it is nothing of the sort. The candidate has taken the view that, because she has identified more advantages than disadvantages, there are good reasons to budget. Evaluation is not simply adding up pros and cons and taking the one from the other to achieve an 'overall' score. Evaluation means a reasoned judgement in the context of the subject and the evidence. Sadly, the candidate does not appear to realise this.

(2) The external things that might affect the management of the nursery are political, economic, social and technical. All of these things happen outside of the business but will affect the business by making it more difficult or easier for the business to operate. The effect of these things will not all be the same so it all really depends on which it is and how much it changes by.

🖉 Although the candidate's use of language is not especially sophisticated, e.g. describing external influences as 'things', the meaning does come through. The use of PEST as a framework is good and this helps to give the answer structure. Another pleasing aspect of the rest of the answer is that the candidate did not feel the need to slavishly write a paragraph on each element of PEST. Remember, with the skills-based marking scheme used on this paper, it is better to develop a few points fully rather than to give lots of weakly reasoned points.

I think one of the biggest changes that will affect the nursery is the number of children being born. Without children being born the nursery will not have enough customers to keep going, so this will be a big influence. From Appendix 4 you can see that the number of children being born falls, then rises and then falls again. From the start to the end the number of children has fallen. Obviously if the number of children being born falls, then the size of the market is getting smaller and so the business will have to fight harder to steal customers and so increase its market share. It could do this by changing its marketing mix and so make the business better than its competitors. To get more customers it might decide to lower its prices from the £500 it charges. Lowering its price means more people will be able to afford to buy and so the business will gain more sales. Before they decide to lower the fee they should work out the PED to see what effect there will be because it might be that the cut in fee might not attract enough new customers to make up for the reduced income they bring in. Another way of gaining more sales is to advertise. Having read the case, I can't see that they do any advertising and so I think they should, as advertising will bring in more customers. In evaluation, advertising might mean costs rise but in the long term income will rise by more than the costs and so advertising is good for the business because the advantages outweigh the disadvantages.

🖉 Having opted to discuss social factors, the candidate's argument is rather simplistic. Why, for example, does she merely describe the movements in the data? Why not pick up a calculator and analyse them? For example, it is possible to show that the number of under 5s falls by 3.9% between 1996 and 2001. Hence, the market the business is aiming at is shrinking, but not particularly quickly. This means the business will have time to adapt strategically to the change. The attempt to link the external change to internal behaviour is good. The candidate has just managed to analyse at this point. The change (falling population) is recognised, its impact (reduced sales) is explained and a consequential change in the operation of the business is given (reduction in fee). Although the quality of the analysis is not great, it would be good enough to gain half marks. The point about price elasticity of demand is sound, but again suffers from the lack of a more fully reasoned discussion.

The other big external thing is the economy. If the economy is doing bad, then the workers in the business will want a pay rise to keep up their spending. This means the business will have to raise its costs so that it can keep profits up because it is a private sector business and so profits are very important. Also, a bad economy will mean that unemployment will go up as more people lose their jobs because businesses shut. From Appendix 1 it is clear that women in work are more likely to use childcare than those who are not economically active. So if unemployment goes up, then the nursery will find that there are fewer people wanting to use it. After all, if you haven't got a job, you can look after your own child and so can save on the £500 it costs to put a baby in a nursery. I think that this is more important than the number of babies being born because it is only mothers in work who need and can afford to use the nursery and so in evaluation the most important thing is the economy.

Discussion of the second environmental influence is appropriate. Again, it is pleasing that the candidate has tried to use the case data to support her position. The link between economic activity and childcare is recognised and this is then reasoned within the context. It is a pity that there was no subsequent discussion of the implication for the strategic management of the business, a clear requirement of the question. Here the skill shown is L2. An external impact has been identified (L1), economic inactivity, and applied (L2) to the situation, falling demand.

This answer illustrates a number of important examination issues. Although the main framework of a good answer is here, the execution is disappointing. It is vital that your written work conveys the full depth of your understanding of the situation. The poor quality of language and poor use of specification vocabulary is evident in the answer. What, exactly, is meant by 'the economy doing bad'? Similarly, does the candidate really believe that the nursery will 'have to raise its costs so that it can keep profits up'? Surely she means price? But the examiner can only mark what is written, and as such the sentence gains no reward because it makes no sense. Overall, this is a weak L3 answer.

(3) Expanding the nursery seems to be a good idea as it has a waiting list. One way to increase profits is to increase revenue by increasing sales, which for this business means taking in more children. This would only be possible with expansion as the nursery is registered to take 26 children and there are 26 names in Appendix 5. This means the nursery is full. The other good thing is that it says that demand for childcare outstrips supply, which means there is a market for more places if Lesley decides to increase the size of the company. There is no point in expanding if there is no demand from the consumer, so Lesley should expand. I think the business should expand on the industrial estate because that is where most working mothers will be working and so they are more likely to use the nursery if it is right nearby. Also, it says that the neighbours are already complaining so if they bought the house next door, then the complaints would only get worse as there would be more children playing and being dropped off by their mothers. If the neighbours complain to the council, then the nursery might not get planning permission to convert the house next door and so the trading estate might be the only alternative. If the business expands, the implications are

they will have to hire more staff and find more money to pay for the rent and nappies and food. The profit in the first three months is very good. The revenue is 95 × £500 = £47,500. The average number of children per member of staff is 5 so she would need 95/5 = 19 staff, which is £14,250 in wages. The feeding and nappy costs average £63.33 per child so that is £6,017. This means the profit will be £106,932. Maybe Lesleys mother can help again, if not the bank might help. If the bank puts the money into the company, then they may want a say in the way it is run in which case Lesley will lose some control.

> ⧉ The good points in the answer are the recognition of two implications: staffing and capital. Unfortunately, these points are not developed sufficiently, so few marks are gained within L2. Although the candidate attempts to analyse the profit generated by the expansion, her analysis is flawed in several respects. Further, the discussion of profit is not linked to strategy and so is tangential to the question set.

Of the three implications I have discussed I think the loss of control is the most important and so in evaluation I think the nursery should expand provided Lesley is able to keep control of her company.

> ⧉ As before, the candidate's attempt at evaluation is unsuccessful. Indeed, there are some fundamental flaws in the logic of the supposed evaluation that betray a lack of understanding about the roles of debt finance and equity finance.
>
> One of the main risks of a pre-seen case study is over-preparing for a question that does not then get asked. Here, it would appear that the candidate was expecting a question about whether the business should expand. Careful reading of the question shows that the main focus is on an associated aspect, the strategic implications of expansion. Another emerging weakness is the poor quality of written communication. Many sentences are long and confusing. There are also grammatical errors, e.g. the failure to use the correct possessive form of Lesley.

(4) Woods and Walker have told Lesley that they want to send a child to the nursery. This is good news for the nursery because it means another customer and so this will mean more profits for the company (see my answer to the other question). Because the profits will have risen, this means that the shareholders will be pleased because they want to get money back on the shares they have invested.

Shareholders are people who own a part of the business and provide the money for it to run. They can vote at the AGM and get dividends from the profits the business makes. The company is a small one and so the shareholders cannot sell their shares on the stock exchange, but if it was a plc they could. The company has limited liability.

> ⧉ This second paragraph lacks relevance and relies too heavily on generalisation. The fact that the final sentence is inaccurate merely compounds the examiner's unease. However, although no marks would be lost, the candidate has wasted her time and contributed to the time pressures she claims to have suffered at the end of the answer.

The objective of all shareholders is to gain money and because more customers means more profits the notice will please them. There won't be any shareholders who won't be pleased. In fact some might want to allow more people from Woods and Walker and so tell Lesley to accept more. This could mean that she has to change the way she runs the business. Change is usually resisted by workers and so Lesley will have to be careful how she makes the changes so she doesn't upset her staff much. But some workers will be pleased as more children will mean Lesley is more likely to expand the business because she knows that profits will rise as this is what she wants. With the company expanding, some workers could get a promotion and rise up Maslow's steps. So in evaluation I think that they will be pleased. Out of time.

This response raises several doubts. First, does the candidate regard stakeholders and shareholders as being one and the same thing? It is possible that shareholders have been used to exemplify the concept of stakeholders. The fact that employees have also been mentioned might give some support to this possibility. In situations like this, where there is uncertainty within an answer, the examiner has to make a judgement. Although the candidate may be given the benefit of the doubt in this case, it is far better not to put yourself in this perilous position. It is good examination practice to start an answer with a definition of the subject-specific vocabulary within the question. Although this may only demonstrate L1, knowledge, it does provide a sound foundation for the rest of the answer. A second concern is that the answer is superficial. It lacks depth and conviction.

The final paragraph is better but is still below the expected standard. The attempt to broaden the discussion beyond shareholders is encouraging but built on a false premise, namely that the business is profit-focused. The point that expansion could be of benefit to employees is valid, but the supporting development is weak. This response would just scrape out of L1 and into L2 by virtue of the weak attempt to apply the concept of stakeholders to the situation and question.

With the exception of Q2, all answers lie within L2. Consistently hitting the top of L2 will, at best, yield a bare pass. Sadly, this candidate mainly operates at the lower end of L2. Even allowing for the weak L3 answer to Q2, the candidate does not amass enough marks. The quality of written communication detracts from the quality of the answer, so full marks would not be awarded for this aspect of the mark scheme either. It is worth noting that the main weakness is not length. Rather it is a lack of focus, with regard to both the subject and the case. Overall, this candidate would be awarded a U grade.

Perfection Plastics Ltd

Perfection Plastics Ltd, manufacturers of injection moulded products, was founded in 1975 by Bob Weston. Tragically Bob was killed in a road traffic accident a couple of years ago, leaving his widow Edith and daughter Jean as the sole owners of the firm. After Bob's death, Edith's initial objective was that the firm should be maintained as 'a going concern' until such time as a realistic sale price could be arranged. Consequently she asked the firm's works manager, George Boardman, to keep the firm 'ticking over' whilst Bob's estate was settled. Although the period after Bob's death was a very difficult time for all of the employees of the firm, George not only kept the firm going, but also managed to secure some new business. As the months passed, Edith gradually began to change her mind and started to form the view that a flourishing firm would be the best possible tribute to her late husband. George and the rest of the workforce were delighted with this positive change of direction and they all started to look to the future with a degree of optimism that had been absent for some time. Everyone at the firm accepted the need for various managerial changes, but there was genuine surprise when Edith announced that Tony Cadnam, her son-in-law, would be leaving the army to become Managing Director.

Although at the time of joining the firm Tony knew very little about injection moulding, he feels his common-sense approach, a willingness to listen to the views of others and the man-management skills he acquired in the army have enabled him to take on the new challenge with some success. Naturally there are still aspects of the running of the business that he realises he has yet to master. However, for a man with no professional training, he feels he is doing a good job!

Injection moulding is, superficially, a straightforward manufacturing process. Plastic granules, stored in a loading hopper, are heated to a paste-like consistency. This paste is injected under great pressure into a cavity between two moulds, called dies. As the material expands into the cavity, it starts to cool and so solidify. When the plastic has acquired the required shape, the two dies are separated. The product is parted from the dies by a small blast of compressed air.

The firm has eight injection moulding machines of various sizes. The pressure exerted on the two dies determines the size of the machine: a 600 tonne(t) machine can hold the two dies together with a force equivalent of up to 600t. The firm's more modern machines, imported from Italy, are computer-controlled. One such 600t machine had a capital cost of £200,000. The computer control facility enables the moulding variables for a particular product to be stored and accessed readily. Variables include the weight of plastic used, temperature settings, injection time, moulding pressure and solidifying time. The last variable depends upon the thickness of the moulding. Settings are decided by George and keyed in by the shift foreman. The next time the machine is set up to make the same product, the necessary machine settings are simply recalled. This facility means that, after the initial set-up variables have been recorded, operating the machine is an unskilled job. George believes that with about

30 minutes of instruction, any adult could be trained to be an operator. An operator working one of the semi-automatic machines is merely required to remove the product from the machine and trim off any excess plastic. As the computer is able to monitor its own statistical compliance with the programmed moulding variables, some products can be produced without the need for continual operator presence. If a machine, running automatically, produces beyond the set limits, it will shut itself down rather than continue to produce defective products.

The firm's main operation is located in a 6,000 sq ft unit on a small industrial estate on the edge of Oakford. In addition it rents another unit nearby. Having two units at different locations causes some problems for the firm. The second unit is used as a storage and packaging facility. The majority of the firm's 39 employees are located at the main unit, with just three at the second site.

Tony and George plan production schedules together. The scheduling meetings involve deciding which machine will make which products and how many of each to make. Sometimes, though, Tony will want to talk matters over with various other people before deciding what is to be done. Typically he consults the sales and administrative staff. Tony believes such consultation supports his view that his style of management is democratic. Tony's approach infuriates George, who resents non-manufacturing staff interfering with his area of responsibility. George would much rather Tony stay in his office and keep off the shop floor. George takes great pride in his belief that, if it is technically possible to design a die to mould a product, he can set up a machine to do it and so allow the firm to take on the work. The moulding dies used by the firm are designed by George in collaboration with a tool-making firm located in the West Midlands, which then manufactures them to the agreed specification. George relishes the intellectual challenge of designing complex moulds. Typically a pair of dies will cost about £80,000 and, if maintained properly, have a virtually unlimited life. As the dies are manufactured from solid metal, they are extremely heavy and so are not easily manoeuvred. Consequently replacing one pair of dies with another pair is a time-consuming business. Further, once the dies have been installed in the machine some fine adjustment is always necessary before production can begin. George reckons that a foreman and tool setter can carry out a die change-over in about 2 hours. The inevitable lost moulding time reduces machine output and hence productive efficiency. George gets upset with anything less than 95% efficiency.

The weekly production schedule and manufacturing specifications of the 600t machine are shown in **Appendix 1**. Deciding how many of each product to make before switching to another is difficult. This week four different products will be made. Two of the products are storage trays whilst a third product is a lid that will fit both the shallow tray and the deep tray. These products are manufactured for stock. A major market for them is schools, with an increasing number now being bought by a major DIY retailer for resale as a general storage product. The fourth product, a seed tray, is part of a £26,000 contract for 20,000 trays from a national garden centre chain. The complete order of seed trays is to be delivered in 4 weeks' time. The customer's payment terms are 60 days after invoice. **Appendix 2** shows the accounts department's costing statement based upon the planned schedule. Tony is concerned that the firm appears to be making a loss on two of its products.

The injection moulding market is competitive and customers are price-sensitive. With this in mind, Tony decided to instigate a night shift 6 months ago in an attempt to gain what he believes are economies of scale. He viewed an additional shift as preferable to the ad hoc overtime previously worked. The firm now operates its machines 24 hours a day, 5 days per week. Weekends are used for planned preventative maintenance. Tony was very pleased with his idea which, literally overnight, increased the firm's productive capacity without the need to engage in a huge capital investment programme. A further advantage of the third shift is the potential increase in productivity as measured by production/man-hour. Shop-floor staffing levels on the night shift reflect the pattern on the two-day shifts and comprise a foreman, a tool setter and five operators. The night shift foreman, Andrew Chapman, volunteered for night shift. He joined the firm 6 years ago as an operator and was promoted to foreman after 5 years. Prior to joining the firm he was a minicab driver. Similarly the tool setter and one operator previously worked days. Three of the new operators were recruited from the local job centre whilst the other four were employed after personal recommendation by existing staff. Traditionally the firm has a high turnover of operators. Tony does not regard this as a problem because the firm has never experienced difficulties in attracting employees.

With the increase in the ability to produce has come an increase in pressure on the sales team to generate new business. Tony is an advocate of a management technique called 'management by objectives' and so believes in setting targets for his subordinates as a means of motivating them. For example, he has told George the required return on capital employed for the 600t machine is 10%. Tony feels it is important that the machines are kept running to meet this figure and so he is loath to turn away any potential business. For example, the firm has recently signed a 2-year contract with a domestic appliance manufacturer to produce moulded vacuum cleaner bodies. In addition, one of the sales staff is negotiating a potential order with a supplier of pet products. This order would be for 10,000 cat litter trays. The trays are a two-piece design. The lower piece has the same dimensions as the shallow storage tray. The upper piece is a removable semi-opaque lid that fits over the lower tray and allows the cat to use the tray without being observed! The lid weighs 700 g. Tony believes the lid could be manufactured within a cycle time of 45 seconds. The labour cost would be 9p per unit whilst running the machine would add a further 50p per unit. Currently the customer imports the litter trays from Germany. The increasing emphasis upon volumes as a strategy for generating revenue is at odds with George's view that the firm should concentrate on technically complex, and hence high-value, mouldings. At least one of the sales team shares his view. Both she and George feel increasingly disaffected.

Whilst it is important that the moulding machines are run constantly, the need for quality control cannot be ignored. **Appendix 3** shows scrap rates. Scrap items usually occur for two main reasons. First the machine may gradually move out of adjustment, for example not injecting enough plastic into each mould. This is known as a 'short shot'. Secondly the operator may not remove the product from the machine in time. Scrap items are cut up on a band saw and then ground into granules. Providing the colour of the old product is light enough, the scrap products can be recycled to make a product of a darker colour. Normally the firm's raw material is clear plastic granules delivered in 25 kg sacks. Clear plastic costs about £650 per tonne. However, as plastic is a product of the petrochemical industry, raw material costs fluctuate with the price of oil. Indeed Tony regards the oil price, measured in $ per barrel, as a leading economic indicator for the firm. To manufacture colour products, pigment granules are mixed in the feed hopper. The amount of pigment to clear plastic will determine the shade produced: 3–5% pigment is typical. Pigment is considerably more expensive than clear plastic, e.g. blue is about £4.89/kg whilst dark brown is £12.95/kg.

Appendix 1 Weekly production schedule, 600t machine

	Lid	Deep tray	Shallow tray	Seed tray	Total
Planned output	4,300	1,650	2,650	1,800	10,400
Cycle time, secs	30	48	30	40	
Max output/hr	120.00	75.00	120.00	90.00	
Time required, hrs	35.83	22.00	22.08	20.00	99.91
Weight, g	300.00	800.00	550.00	400.00	

Appendix 2 Costing statement, £, 600t machine

	Lid	Deep tray	Shallow tray	Seed tray	Total
Revenue	3,225.00	4,950.00	5,300.00	2,340.00	15,815.00
Direct costs					
Material	838.50	858.00	947.38	468.00	3,111.88
Machine running	1,433.33	880.00	883.33	800.00	3,996.66
Labour	357.23	137.08	220.15	149.54	864.00
Indirect costs					
Labour	1,240.38	475.96	764.42	519.24	3,000.00
Capital	347.31	133.27	214.03	145.39	840.00
Maintenance etc.	62.02	23.80	38.22	25.96	150.00
Selling and administration	1,259.00	483.10	775.88	527.02	3,045.00
Profit/(loss)	(2,312.77)	1,958.79	1,456.59	(295.15)	807.46

Appendix 3 Scrap rates by shift

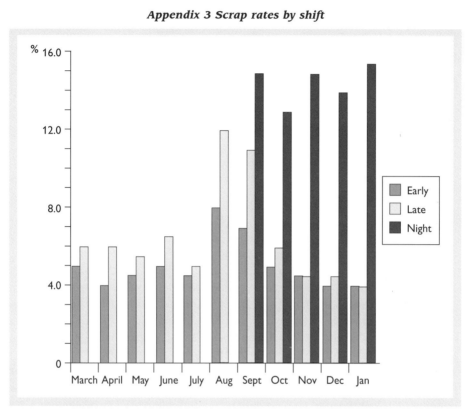

Answer all questions

(1) Critically assess the effectiveness of the management of change at
Perfection Plastics. (18 marks)

(2) Tony is deciding whether to expand the business's product portfolio. Discuss to
what extent analytical tools, such as Ansoff's matrix, might assist him in making
the decision whether to accept the order for the cat litter trays. (19 marks)

(3) Evaluate how changes in the sterling exchange rate may affect Perfection
Plastics's strategic behaviour. (19 marks)

(4) One of the business's strategic objectives is for 10% return on capital. Discuss
how Tony might ensure the business achieves this objective. (20 marks)

Total: 76 marks

■ ■ ■

Answer to case study 2: candidate A

(1) Change is an inevitable aspect of business. The change may occur in the business's
external environment or within the business itself. Faced with change, those
managing the business need to reassess their SWOT analysis to see if the business
is still able to achieve its objectives. This can only be done if the firm has the right
resources and these are arranged so that the business's strengths match the

environmental opportunities. If the business does not have the right resources, or the right ones are doing the wrong thing, then change will be necessary to get the business headed back in the right direction. The four steps to planning change are planning, implementation, control and finally review. Each stage has to be properly managed if the business is to emerge from the change able to succeed.

> ℮ This is a very impressive start but, given the skills-based marking strategy used, it does not score highly. Whilst it may appear to be full of good material, it does not refer to the business in question and as such it is not in the context of the case study. The strength of the paragraph is, however, to focus on the question — this sets a good foundation for the application of understanding to the case later in the answer.

The problem for Perfection Plastics (PP) is that the change, Bob Weston's death, was not anticipated and it was beyond the control of the business because no one wanted the actual change to take place. After Bob's death there was really no one in charge of the business to undertake the change process. Although the business carried on, because it is a company its life is independent of its owners, the two owners, Edith and Jean, didn't really know how to run the business or what to do. They originally thought they would sell and so during this time the business's objectives would have been survival until a sale could be arranged. However, because of a change in stakeholder objectives, this business objective changed to one of growth after the appointment of Tony as MD. With Tony now in charge, the business has emerged from the change as a successful business. But I don't think the change process was actually managed. The owners of the business did not plan the eventual change; rather they let George take over the operation of the business whilst they sorted out their ideas. However, it is not clear whether George managed the change either. He seems to have tried to keep the business going rather than change its direction. So, his role was more one of maintenance than change. Having been successful in this, he is now becoming frustrated that, having been given the opportunity to run the business, this was taken away from him. It is clear that George is becoming increasingly frustrated and is starting to under-mine Tony in his efforts to run the business.

> ℮ This paragraph begins in a strongly analytical vein. The candidate gives a fully reasoned discussion of the situation the business is facing at this key time in its development. The candidate adopts an evaluative stance: having analysed the situation, she shares her doubt with the reader and suggests that, whilst what happened is indeed 'change', it has not been managed because it does not conform to the accepted model of strategic management of change.

After taking over the business, Tony has started to make some changes. These he is doing gradually and so these changes are within the control of the business. For example, Tony has changed working methods and introduced a night shift. He has also tried to change the culture of the business to one of growth and expansion by placing emphasis on volumes. In doing this the process of change is being managed. Tony has planned what he wants to do and consults with his staff about it. This consultation will help to overcome some of the natural resistance to change that all people, especially older people, have. Tony has then implemented the changes he wants, and has hired new workers to achieve this. His target was to increase volumes and this has been achieved by taking new orders. However, it is not a very good aim because it doesn't conform to the SMART model. At the moment they are in the review phase of the process. From the scrap rates it seems that the process has not been fully achieved yet. Also, George is still not happy and so Tony hasn't managed to fully change the culture of the organisation because a key member of it is still clinging to the old ways.

Tony has managed the change of PP quite well. Having been thrown in the deep end, he has kept the business going. Now that he is more confident, he is making necessary changes and the business is flourishing. If this is to continue I think he needs to sack George because George is resistant to change and he wants the business to stay the same. Unless George is sacked, Tony's good management of change will be undermined.

✍ The remaining paragraphs are sound but do not revisit the evaluation seen in the second one. Much of the rest of the answer shows a confident ability to apply the model learnt. There is some weak analysis within these parts, but no additional marks are awarded as the skill being shown is lower than that already seen. Overall, this is a good answer which would secure the majority of the marks.

(2) Ansoff's matrix is an analytical tool which helps managers assess the degree of risk associated with different strategic decisions regarding products and markets. It has four squares:

	Existing product	New product
Existing market	Market penetration	Product development
New market	Market extension	Diversification

The more the business moves away from its current position, existing product to an existing market, the greater the risk it is taking. If a greater risk is taken, then the business needs to be making a higher level of profit to compensate. Also, if they start to take extra risks with one new product or one new market, they need to be sure that this is balanced by good profits from their current business just in case the new venture goes wrong.

✍ This answer gets off to a good start by focusing clearly on the main aspect of the question: Ansoff's matrix. However, this first paragraph is in the abstract; there is no linkage to the case study so it would only be awarded at L1.

It is not easy to fit the new order into Ansoff's matrix. It seems the customer is new, so there is risk there because it is either market extension or diversification. The base is an existing product (market extension), but the lid is new (diversification). So it is clear that Ansoff is not that useful because of the confusion about which square the order fits in. But it is useful in that Tony will know he is facing a greater risk than if he just carries on as he is. So Tony, being aware of this risk, might decide only to take this one new order and no others until he has successfully managed the extra risk. In other words, he should not risk too much on too many new ideas all at once.

📝 This and subsequent paragraphs apply the concept to the situation. The discussion regarding the uncertainty of how Ansoff can be applied is good and demonstrates a sound appreciation of the concept. The fact that the use of Ansoff is then credited with a change in behaviour (awareness of risk limiting the taking on of too many new ideas at once) is enough to gain L3.

An alternative view is that the lid is not really that much of a new product. It is, after all, much the same as the products they currently make, with the machinery and workers they have (injection moulded plastic), and so they have the resources to do it. So, the lid isn't really a big diversification, unlike that which George wants to do with complex shapes. In which case the order is market extension according to Ansoff.

📝 The analysis of the business's resources in this paragraph reinforces L3.

Tony should be using other tools when making this decision. He should be doing a CPA and a forecast about the market to see if it's going to grow. He could also use a decision tree here because that would help him. So analytical tools are a good thing to use, but Ansoff's matrix is not the only one to think about.

📝 The final paragraph suggests that the candidate reread the question and thought it sensible to identify other analytical tools. Whilst this adds further depth to the answer, it does not add to the marks awarded as there is no improvement on the skill already shown. Overall, this is a mid-L3 response.

(3) A change in the value of sterling is an external influence on the business over which it has no control. As an analysis of the external environment is a major influence on strategic decisions, such a change may well cause the business to reassess its plans and to behave in a different way. But external change is not the only consideration — the business also needs to think about the internal resources it has and the different stakeholders of the business it is trying to please. So a change in the value of sterling may in fact not affect PP's strategic behaviour.

📝 A good start that serves to show the examiner that the candidate understands the linkage between strategy and environment.

As the question is not clear which way the pound has moved, I will assume that changes in the sterling exchange rate mean a fall in the value of the pound against other currencies. If the pound were to rise, the effect would be the opposite. A falling pound means that the pound price of imported goods rises and the price of exports falls. PP makes plastic containers and so one of their big costs is raw material. The plastic comes from crude oil and so a fall in the pound will mean a pound rise in oil costs and in turn an increase in PP's raw material costs. This will encourage PP to want to raise their price to compensate and so maintain profit. The problem is that this might mean fewer customers, as we know the customers are price sensitive. So increasing prices will cause demand to fall and customers to buy from other plastic firms. But one good thing for PP is that the increase in raw materials will be the same for all plastic businesses and so they will all want to raise price. If they all do this, then the customers will not be able to save money by shopping around because all prices have risen. So it could be that PP will not lose any business. In fact, if Tony can gauge the market right, he might even benefit by buying lots of raw materials now before the pound falls. This would give him a cheaper stockpile of plastic than his competitors and so when they raise price, he wouldn't have to. But this is risky because he might guess the market incorrectly. The other problem is that increasing stocks is expensive and this extra expense might be more than the cost saving of stock piling. So before Tony does this he would need to work it all out very carefully.

🖉 The assumption made at the start of this second paragraph is perfectly acceptable — if you can argue the case for a decrease, there is no point in repeating the argument in reverse by discussing a rise in sterling. This paragraph shows a clear appreciation of the impact of the given external change on the firm. The only issue is whether the answer addresses the notion of 'strategic behaviour' as required by the question. There is clear analysis of the impact but not much to suggest how this would change the strategic direction of the business.

The other way that PP will be affected is buying new machinery or parts for their machines. The machines they use are imported from Italy and so a fall in the value of the pound will mean the capital costs of their machines will rise. This makes buying the machines cost more and so might discourage PP from investing. Higher capital costs will increase the amount they might have to borrow and so the amount of interest they have to pay will go up. This will mean higher costs in the profit and loss account and so a fall in profits. But the decision to buy a new piece of capital equipment would not depend solely on the exchange rate. Other things would also be important such as the future demand for the products the machine can make. Also, if PP is committed to enter a new market or has a new customer, then it might have to buy the machine anyway regardless of its cost. Also, just because the pound has fallen doesn't mean the cost of the machine will go up because the importer might decide not to pass on this extra amount. If the value of sterling has been fluctuating a lot, then the importer may well decide to keep prices constant and even out any movement rather than confuse the customer by constantly changing the price.

🖉 The candidate now makes a clear link between the change and strategy. This is done by the reasoned view that plans for expansion, a clear strategic issue, would not be wholly dependent upon the identified change. This demonstrates L4.

The impact of a change in the sterling exchange rate on PP will depend upon how big the movement is, whether it is sustained and whether it was anticipated or not. Small, one-off movements up and down will probably not cause the business to reassess its strategy. However, large-scale falls over a long period of time might well cause them to rethink their strategy. For example, a big fall in the value of sterling might make them reassess expansion plans given the additional capital costs because of the imported machinery. Without clear information about the changes, it is not really possible to say how PP will react.

This concluding paragraph, combined with the third, ensures that the response reaches L4. Overall, this is a very good answer.

(4) A strategic objective is one that sets the overall direction of the business for quite some period of time. In setting strategic objectives, managers need to be aware of what the company's different stakeholders expect from the business and how they will react to any objective set. Strategic objectives correspond to the business's overall mission statement and show where the business is headed. This communication of direction serves to inform everyone associated with the business as to their role and how what they do is important to the overall success of the business. By knowing the strategic direction of the business, employees will be motivated to work harder to achieve. Objectives form the basis for the setting of targets, which are often described as being SMART. Targets also act as a motivator, especially if the employees have had a role in setting them.

The candidate begins with an opening paragraph that addresses the concept in the question. Although abstract, this serves to focus both writer and reader.

Because Tony is an advocate of management by objectives, it is fair to assume that employee participation in target setting happens in PP. This means that employees, by being involved in target setting, will know exactly what is required of them so they know what they need to achieve. Also, because of their involvement in setting targets, they will feel a sense of ownership and so be more committed to the targets. If the targets had merely been imposed, then they may well have said the targets are too difficult and so not bothered about trying to achieve them, feeling their efforts would be wasted working towards an impossible target. By involving the employees in the setting of targets it is far more likely the target set will be achieved. So one way that Tony can achieve the target is through his employees, by establishing a culture of employee participation so that motivation levels are high.

One problem is that Tony may not actually involve his employees in target setting. It is said that Tony likes to 'talk matters through before deciding what is to be done'. This implies that although he communicates with his staff, he may not in fact be creating a participative culture. It could be that Tony only feels he should listen to his staff because that is what a good democratic manager will do. Although Tony likes to think of himself being a democratic manager, there is evidence that he is autocratic because he doesn't act on the views he receives.

This may make the staff feel demotivated as they are being conned into thinking their views matter whereas Tony has in fact already decided what to do. In effect he is engaging in pseudo-participation. It appears that George has already come to this view as he resents non-production staff being involved. This problem is reinforced when it says that he has 'told' George. Also we are told earlier that Tony 'decided' to instigate a night shift. There is no evidence to support the possibility that Tony consulted widely on this major decision.

> The candidate demonstrates clear analysis in these paragraphs through linking the achievement of objectives with employees. The discussion comparing Tony's perceived leadership style with the reality is good and well supported by the use of case material.

Return on capital is a financial objective. So, another way Tony can achieve this objective is by ensuring the business gains enough revenue to cover its costs. One issue which is hampering gaining enough profit is the high scrap rates, particularly on the night shift. The problem with scrap rates is that the business is paying to produce items which it cannot sell, so it is having costs which aren't balanced by revenues. Although they are able to recycle some of the scrap to save raw material costs, it would be far better to avoid scrap in the first place. So in order to achieve the objective, Tony needs to sort out the quality problems they are having. This could be done by having a meeting with Andrew Chapman and seeing what the problem is. Because Andrew is experienced and two of the other staff on nights are, then it is most likely that the new people are not working properly. So Andrew needs to be told to supervise them more closely until they are more able to work alone without making lots of scrap items. If the other two shifts can manage to keep their scrap levels down, then so should the night shift.

> By addressing scrap rates and again drawing on the case evidence, the answer is clearly within the context and focused on the question.

To evaluate, I think the way that Tony can achieve his objective is through his employees. The employees are the most important stakeholders the business has because without employees there is no business. Tony needs to make sure everyone is aware of what they need to do. If necessary he should get rid of George because I feel George is a troublemaker because he didn't get Tony's job.

> The final paragraph is weak and may reflect time pressures. However, whilst sympathetic, the examiner cannot award marks on this basis. Is there evaluation in the answer? Unfortunately not, and so top L3 marks would be awarded.

> **Overall, the candidate would gain a grade A. The responses demonstrate a mixture of top analysis and evaluation. The candidate's use of the case material is good throughout and is blended well with a clear grasp of the subject. The candidate develops the responses fully, but the answer and critique to Q1 show that length is not essential.**

Answer to case study 2: candidate B

(1) Tony has managed the changes at Perfection Plastics, which I will call PP from now on. Since he has taken over the business it has grown and is doing well. He has taken on more staff and the business is doing more business than before now that there is a night shift as well as the two day shifts. Effectiveness is measured by whether the business has reached the objectives set for it. Without a clear objective it is not possible to say whether what the business is doing is effective or not because without an objective there is no goal to aim for or to measure performance against. If Tony's idea of making the business bigger is the aim, then yes the process has been managed effectively. But if he has some other objective, then the process hasn't been done well.

> 🖉 This is not an easy answer to assess. The candidate has clearly been made aware of the need to offer a two-sided argument in order to achieve L4. This is apparent in the opening paragraph with the 'on the one hand, but on the other' style of discussion. It might be tempting to argue that this is a balanced discussion leading to a conclusion. The problem is that it is tangential to the question set. There is no recognition of the need to consider the management of change, the key business studies concept within the question. Instead, the candidate has decided to answer the question 'Is Tony doing a good job at PP?' Although the answer is balanced, it would not gain any marks.

One problem is that although the business is now growing by taking on more volume, not all of this is profitable. Even Tony has seen that on two out of four products the business is making a loss. Altogether the business is making £807.46 profit, which is good, but the business could be doing better. But Tony mustn't stop making the two loss-making products because they are both making a contribution of £595.94 and £922.46 each. If he stopped these two products, the firm's profit would become a £710.94 loss because the indirect costs would still need to be paid. So what Tony needs to do to be more effective is to find more profitable business rather than just any business. But before turning down business, Tony needs to think about his cash flow because whether the machines are running or not he will be paying out cash and so it is important that he has a steady inflow to match this. Even if this means taking some loss-making business, then he should to gain cash.

> 🖉 The second paragraph continues in much the same way. Here the candidate is very adept at bringing his understanding of contribution to bear on the case so that he can answer another question of his own making, possibly 'Should PP discontinue making seed trays?'

In evaluation, Tony is effective in his management of PP. PP is a private limited company and so will be aiming to make a profit and, from Appendix 2, we can see he is doing this. Although he has some staff turnover, this is not a problem because they always attract new staff without any problem. If he could reduce staff turnover, then he would be doing even better.

🖉 The final paragraph seeks to act as an evaluative summary. Sadly, it fails in this task in that, by introducing new material, it doesn't actually summarise. Further, it is not evaluative. So, what mark should be awarded? Does the answer contain evaluation? No, so it is not L4. Does it contain analysis? Yes, but the analysis is not relevant to the question set, so it is not L3 either. Is there application of the management of change within the context of PP? Again, the answer is 'no' and so L2 cannot be awarded. Finally, having come all the way down the levels of response, is there demonstration of knowledge of the management of change in PP? Regrettably not, and consequently the answer would be awarded no marks.

(2) The order for cat litter trays is an example of market extension according to Ansoff's matrix because they are selling an existing product to a new customer. This means that there is increased risk because although they know about the product, they do not know about the customer. But all business is a risk and to accumulate you have to speculate, and so Tony shouldn't worry a lot about this.

🖉 In this opening paragraph the candidate demonstrates his knowledge of Ansoff's matrix through the use of appropriate vocabulary (market extension). The fact that there is some attempt to apply this to the situation by describing the litter tray as an existing product is just enough to gain L2.

The order is for 10,000 trays. The bottom part is the same as the shallow tray they already make. This takes them 30 seconds and makes them £0.55 profit on each one according to Appendices 1 and 2. To make the lid will take 45 seconds, and so they can make 80 per hour. So the entire order will take 125 hours for the lids and 83.3 hours for the bases. The cost of the clear plastic for the lid is £4,550. The shading can be from recycled coloured scrap. The machine time costs £40 per hour, so that makes £5,000. The cost of direct labour depends upon the production schedule as labour is charged as a proportion of total output, but it averages as £8.65 per hour so the entire order will cost £1,081.25. So the total direct cost is £10,631.25. The shallow trays will cost £14,503.43, making the total order cost £25,134.86, or about £2.52 per litter tray.

So if Tony can get the new customer to pay more than £2.52 per tray, then he should take the order. This type of product is exactly what Tony wants to aim for as it is a simple product and so will increase the throughput of the business and so increase volumes in line with his objective of getting new business. Tony can also say to the customer his price is guaranteed and independent of the pound against the euro, which is a risk the customer takes at the moment as the product is imported. This could be a big plus for the customer. Tony should also emphasise quality and that PP is a reliable supplier.

🖉 These paragraphs demonstrate some sophisticated quantitative analysis that reflects the candidate's good understanding of the material in the pre-seen material. However, the candidate has not applied this analysis to the question asked, so the answer could not be highly rewarded. The candidate has addressed the issue as to whether the order should be accepted, but the question asked was about the usefulness of analytical tools.

In evaluation, whether he should accept the order depends upon the price the customer is prepared to pay. If it is more than £2.52, he should.

Given that much of the answer is irrelevant to the question about the usefulness of analytical tools, the only part that could be rewarded is the first paragraph. To score high marks your answer must be relevant to the question set. One peril of a pre-seen case is that you may prepare for a question that does not get asked.

(3) The sterling exchange rate is a measure of how much foreign currency can be bought for £1. A rise in the exchange rate will mean that you can buy more foreign currency with the same amount of sterling because the pound becomes worth more; it rises against other currencies. A rise in sterling means that UK exports become less price competitive in foreign markets and so, according to the laws of supply and demand, the number sold will fall. So a rise in sterling is bad for exporters. But it is good for importers because now the same number of pounds can buy more foreign goods and so the price of these can fall in the UK, meaning that the numbers sold will rise, so allowing the importer to make more profits.

This opening paragraph sets the scene well.

Nowhere in the case does it mention that PP exports, and so it appears that they need not be concerned with exchange rates. But because Tony regards the oil price as being a leading indicator, this view is not quite true. The price of oil is measured in dollars per barrel and so if the pound rises against the dollar, then it will mean the pound price of oil will fall. This will in turn mean the price of PP's raw material, plastic, will fall because plastic is produced from the petrochemical industry. This means that PP's costs will fall. From Appendix 2 we can see that raw materials are 20.7% of total cost. If a rise in the pound means materials become 10% cheaper, then PP would save about 2% of total cost. With lower costs PP can do one of two things. First, they could keep their prices constant and so make more profit on each product sold. This would be good for them as they are a limited company and so profit will be a key objective. The other thing they could do is keep their profit margin and lower price. Because the market is price-sensitive, a cut in price will lead to a bigger rise in demand and, according to the laws of economics, revenue will rise. This is good for the business as, with the same profit being made on each unit and selling more units, their profits will rise.

The candidate makes very good use of the case material in this paragraph. His willingness and ability to use the numerate information is good and quickly enables the answer to be seen as analytical. However, in undertaking this numerate analysis of the case material the candidate merely offers the outcome. It is good examination technique to show how the outcome is achieved. For example, how is the raw material context of 20.7% arrived at? If the value quoted had not been correct, the examiner would have had to regard it as an attempt to apply case evidence to the situation, L2. Since it is correct, it is analysis, L3. But missing out method is too big a risk to take.

A rise in the value of the pound will mean that imports into the UK become cheaper. If the plastic tray market suffers from imports, then PP will have to fight off these cheaper imports. But I don't think this is a problem for them because it doesn't say anything in the case about imported goods. Also, the value of their products is low and so it is probably not worth importing them. The seed tray, for example, has a price of £1.30 and weighs 0.4 kg. It seems unlikely that with the costs of transporting added to the manufacturing costs, an imported seed tray could be sold for much less than PP can make them for in the UK. There would have to be a really big rise in the pound for this to be true, so I don't think Tony needs to worry about imports.

✍ The quality of the analysis in this answer is good. This is evident in the discussion in this paragraph to support the view that imports are not an issue. This is an aspect of the case that is unclear but, by virtue of his reasoning, the candidate's view can be accepted.

To evaluate a rise in the value of the pound would be good for PP as their costs fall. There are no bad things with a rise in the pound and so it will be good for the business. The opposite would be true if the pound fell. So my evaluation is that whether it is good or not depends upon whether the pound rises or falls.

✍ The candidate needs to demonstrate evaluation to move the marks beyond L3 into L4. Does the final paragraph do this? Unfortunately, it adds nothing in terms of skill shown and consequently the answer remains at L3.

(4) Return on capital is a common business objective and a sensible one for Tony to have for the business. It compares the profit made by the business to the amount of money invested in it. Knowing this, the owners can decide whether the business is doing well by comparing their ROC with the interest rates in the bank. Ideally ROC should be above bank interest rates; otherwise the owners' money would be better off in the risk-free bank account rather than being exposed to the risk in running the business.

From Appendix 2 we can see that the business makes £807.46 profit in a week using the 600t machine. Assuming a 48-week year, this is yearly profit of £38,758. This machine cost £200,000 and so its return on capital is 19.4%. This is almost double the required return that Tony has set and suggests the business will have little difficulty in achieving his objective. In fact, this could work against Tony because staff may see this objective as being too easy and so reduce their efforts. For example, they might think 'why should we bother about the time it takes to swap the machines over because we are making a lot of profit going slowly'. Also, they might not get too concerned about scrap rates. Even if Tony includes the £80,000 capital cost of the dies in his calculation, then ROC is still 13.8%, over a third higher than his target. So, it seems that Tony can achieve the target he has set, although he needs to guard against complacency amongst his staff. Maybe he should review the target upwards to make it a bit more realistic.

It is clear that this candidate feels equally at ease with numerate and verbal information. What is especially pleasing is the use of number, although there is no explicit requirement to engage in this behaviour. These paragraphs demonstrate sound analysis.

One problem with the calculation is that it assumes Appendix 2 is typical of the weekly performance of the business. It could be that this week is a busy one and so profit levels might be higher. Another problem is that this machine is a good one but the others are not so good. So although this machine hits the objectives, the other seven machines might be less efficient and so the overall value for the whole business could well be a lot lower. Another big worry is that the machine is producing 1,800 seed trays at a loss of £295.15. This means the total order of 20,000 trays will make a loss of £3,279.44. So Tony is accepting orders which make a loss and if he carries on doing this he cannot achieve his 10% objective. The only way that he might is if this order is being used as a way of securing more profitable business in the future. But because it says the market is price sensitive, it is unlikely the business can raise price without the customer going to a cheaper competitor. After all, a plastic tray is a plastic tray, and so PP are unlikely to be able to create brand loyalty.

 Having established the view that the 10% objective is easily met, the candidate now begins to reason that it may not be so easy after all. This counterpoint sets up the evaluative view about the target (remember, evaluation is a reasoned argument in the context of the case). This evaluation means top marks would be awarded.

In evaluation, Tony can achieve the objective by making sure his business is run efficiently. This means his staff need to be motivated and capable of doing their jobs. For example, the production staff have to run the machines well. Also the sales staff need to make sure any orders they accept are profitable. Although Tony feels he is doing a good job, he has to be aware that taking any order that comes along is not always the best way to ensure objectives are met.

 The multidisciplinary approach taken in the final paragraph, which suggests that the achievement of the objective requires attention to both motivation (HRM) and accepting business, is good: it considers both marketing and finance issues.

 Overall, the candidate would be awarded a grade E. The main reason for this is that two of the answers are not sufficiently focused on the question set. Indeed, the first would not gain any marks. The key learning point here is the need to be rigorous in reading the question set and ensuring this is the one answered. By the end of Q2 the candidate would have achieved less than 15% of the available marks. This is not because he cannot engage in higher-order skills but because he does not answer the questions set.

The fact that the remaining two answers are good lifts the overall standard of the answer. On these last two questions the candidate would be awarded enough marks for a top B or low A. It is a pity that this higher standard is not evident throughout the script.